Y0-BCO-332

1 – 5 + 10 + 15 + 20 = THE RIGHT JOB

1 − 5 + 10 + 15 + 20 = THE RIGHT JOB

PHYLLIS MARTIN

St. Martin's Press • New York

This book is dedicated to:
Every job seeker everywhere—but especially to those I wanted to hire and couldn't. Did you know that a part of me went with you as you left? You see, there was so much I wanted to say.

and

The friends, the family and others around the job seeker. You can do so much and undo so much in your job seeker's campaign. This book tells you how to make job seeking a bright, positive experience for that someone who matters to you.

 For information, write:
St. Martin's Press, Inc., 175 Fifth Avenue, New York, N.Y. 10010
Manufactured in the United States of America

Library of Congress Cataloging in Publication Data

Martin, Phyllis Rodgers.
Martin's Magic formula for getting the right job.

1. Job hunting—United States. 2. Vocational guidance—United States. I. Title
HF5382.75.U6M37 650.1'4 80-29156
ISBN 0-312-51702-5
ISBN 0-312-51703-3 (pbk.)

10 9 8 7 6 5 4 3 2 1

First Edition

CONTENTS

ACKNOWLEDGMENTS

A special thanks to Barbara Anderson, my editor at St. Martin's Press. Somehow Barbara managed to be both incisive and sensitive. I love this book and I appreciate her improving it while maintaining the essence and spirit of it.

Thanks also to my husband, Bruce, to my daughter, Shirlie, to Charles Beaty II, Leo Hirtl, Jill Baker, Mindy Welch, Marycarol Barnes, Joseph Tinervia, Alan C. Lloyd, Jennifer Jolly-Ryan, Lee Cordray, Linda Mears, and Marjorie McKinney.

And to the countless job seekers who shared the experiences of their search with me.

FOREWORD

No one wants to go through the brutally hard work of writing *a book. Certainly I didn't.*

Then why this book?

All right, I'll tell you. I wanted to have written *a book that describes a process I've developed for creative job seeking. If I could have found certain elements of my process (I call it Martin's Magic Formula) in other job books now on the market, I wouldn't have tied myself to this task. But so many critical factors were not included in these other books. Factors such as:*

- turning that old devil "no experience" into a positive technique
- turning rejection from a downer into an exhilarating part of the campaign
- recognizing that how you sound is every inch as important as how you look and providing a means for ridding the vocabulary of "wince" words
- lifting the interest of other family members from a level of, shall we say, interference to that of significant contribution
- focusing the attention on some of the tiny, tiny factors that actually make the difference between a turndown and a job offer. (Example: make a copy of the application form. Practice filling out the copy before you tackle the real one. You'll not only produce a neater application, but you'll have a permanent record of what you told the prospective employer.)

I wrote the book for another compelling reason: I have orders for it—orders from organizations and the promise of orders from many job counselors and teachers. One of the most persistent inquirers, Charles Beaty II, called countless times to ask, "May I use those rating sheets you developed? How about writing down what you told my students about rejection? How does the magic formula go again? When *are* you going to write that book?"

Actually, this book started some time ago—on the day I first had to say no to a job seeker. I believe something happened inside me that day, and despite having conducted some fifty thousand job interviews that same feeling remains. Often I ached to say, "Oh, if only you'd done such and such," or "If you hadn't done such and such, I would have hired you." I began to make notes in case some of the smarter applicants asked for tips.

After I left my job as personnel counselor for the Procter & Gamble Company (to marry a P&G man), I couldn't shake the habit of working with job seekers. And I couldn't shake the habit of writing down the tips and guidelines I'd gathered from my work. I began a career column with the meatiest of these tips, and before long the column developed into question-and-answer sessions with job seekers via newspapers, television, and face-to-face sessions.

As I write this I realize I seem to have moved all the way around the desk. I'm not content to stay on the interviewer's side anymore; I'm with the job seeker. Every day I write about jobs, every day I plot a job campaign with someone, and every week I usually schedule two or more talks with job-bound groups at schools, colleges, and universities as well as with organizations.

So, if you're thinking about a job when you leave school, if you're reentering the job market, or even if you're a careerist who's changing jobs, let me go along with you to show you my method. If you were dieting, you'd follow a diet. If you're job hunting, you need a method, which is what this book is all about.

Follow this guide, manual, method—or magic formula. It works.

INTRODUCTION

Martin's Magic Formula
1 - 5 + 10 + 15 + 20 = 5 Job Offers

Martin's Magic Formula is built around a basic magic formula. That word *magic* has been used so often that I hesitated using it for a while. But it's now an established part of my program because so many job seekers who tried the formula declared that it works like magic. Yes, it even worked for those who came to me with queasy stomachs, sweaty palms, or giant inferiority complexes.

Here are the instructions for building a soaringly successful job campaign.

Special Note: If you are a so-called handicapped person—hearing-impaired, physically disabled—or if you have a special problem, you will need to follow this procedure a second or a third time. But don't give up. It works.

Martin's Magic Formula
1 −5 + 10 + 15 + 20 = 5 job offers.
Reduce the five offers to one acceptance.

1. Start with the number 1. This stands for *one job seeker—You.* You, dressed in an absolutely smashing (but conservative) job-seeking outfit, wearing a smile—a smile that reflects a good attitude. Go in hock for the outfit if you must. (For an explanation of "Packaging the Product," see page 12.)

−5. Now delete five. Five what? You delete five abused or misused words from your vocabulary. Not using undesirable words is an often overlooked but critical factor. It is important to every job seeker. (Yes, the Ph.D. candidate as well.)

Ideally, you should eliminate all incorrect and abused words, but let's settle for the five most irritating ones. For help with this, turn to "Help for 'Hear'-Ache" on page 75.

+10. This stands for ten questions (five prospective-employer questions and five applicant questions). Every interview is a question-and-answer game. Learn to play it.

Study the segment on questions, page 57. Then close the book and rattle off at least five questions that an interviewer might ask. Practice answering the questions. Next, rattle off at least five appropriate questions for you to ask the interviewer.

+15. Whether it's asked or not, the question in every interviewer's mind is this one: Why should I hire you? In order to answer this question, you'll need to have on tap at least fifteen reasons why you'd be an asset to an organization. Reasons such as your ability to organize projects, your ability to save the company money, your energy, your ability to get along with others, your ability to set priorities, your creativity, your sense of responsibility, your skills (such as blueprint reading, knowledge of computers, typing, your ability to handle machinery, and so on).

Your reasons will be different from anyone else's. When you have developed *your* list, test yourself by having someone time you as you enumerate your reasons aloud. You have mastered this exercise when you can tick off fifteen reasons in as many seconds. No, don't memorize them but store them in the computer that is your brain. That way at least four or five of these reasons will spill out of you at interview time, no matter how nervous you are. The segment "You Are You-nique," page 8, will help you in this exercise.

An added bonus is this: The exercise will help you to develop a strong résumé if one is required.

+20. The number 20 refers to twenty interviews with prospective employers. You need to make *at least* twenty solid interviews before you can expect to have five job offers. Please study "The Territory" section, page 18, for help in developing your list of prospects. Also, read about "How to Turn Rejection Into Positive Direction" on page 101. In particular, think about the concept that you cannot leave any interview empty-handed if you want the magic formula to work.

Now, please read the entire book. Every page contains at least one pearl. Look for them. Good hunting.

PART I

The Job Search

CHAPTER 1

You are You-nique

Perhaps you are thinking, "Why me? Why do I need advice about applying for a job?" Maybe you don't. But then, if you're like the average "Jo," or "Joe," maybe you do because you do the most miserable job of selling the most important product you'll ever sell—yourself.

"Why is that?" you say.

Because applying for a job doesn't strike most people as a selling job. It is.

If you forget everything else about this book, please remember these two points:

1. When you apply for a job you become a salesperson—with you as the product.
2. The employment interviewer is the purchasing agent for the company. She or he must buy the best possible product for the money available. And your paycheck, even if it is modest, represents a big expenditure. If you add your weekly salary up to obtain a yearly figure, it always comes out to be thousands of dollars.

Would you just give jobs to people because they asked? Of course not. Not for very long you wouldn't. Nor will that purchasing agent we call the personnel interviewer.

Now then, we've settled the part about what it is you're really doing when you apply for a job. Pretend for a moment that you are the job interviewer. Close your eyes. Let me be the job applicant making the rounds.

I come in and gulp, "Hello."

I don't call you by name. I haven't bothered to learn it.

I don't know what your company makes or does (but you're supposed to be impressed because I do know I want a job with you).

I don't know whether I'm in the home office, sales office, branch office, or *where* I am.

When you ask what kind of work I want to do, I shrug and say, "I dunno. Anything, I guess."

Now I'm sore because you won't hire me.

Worse still, you don't level with me. You merely say, "Sorry, we have no suitable opening."

"Yeah, I hear that everywhere I go," I mumble as I shuffle out your office door.

A dreary scene? Yes.

So let's change the scene as well as the script. Let's recognize that *there are jobs available* right now, though it *is* hard work to find a good one.

If you're willing to do the work of finding work, but just don't know how to go about it, read on.

The scene opens to an employment office.

You're in the waiting room. Waiting.

Applicants who have been there before you say they were scared, frustrated, nervous, angry, exhausted; that they had burning eyes, sweaty palms, tired feet; that they were chicken to go in that door.

If you identify with any of these emotions, your situation is not unique.

But you are.

What makes you so you-nique?

You have a combination of characteristics unlike anyone else's in the world. When you discover the factors that go together to make you *you,* you'll have made a start toward describing the product that is you—the product you hope to sell to a prospective employer.

Put Yourself Into a Neat Package

First, let's take a look at the product being sold. The prospective employer certainly will. How have you packaged the product that is you?

"If they don't like the way I look, I don't want to work there anyway." Have you heard anyone voice this sentiment? I have, very recently.

Yet the young man who expressed this feeling was willing to spend hours preparing his jacked-up Nova for sale. Of course, he used chrome cleaner, soap and water, spit and polish—the works.

"Why," I asked him, "is your Nova worth more than you are?"

Now I ask you a similar question: Why won't you spend as much time getting yourself ready for the sale as you would in preparing any other product?

Consider for a minute the human being who will be on the other side of the desk when you have your job interview. That human being—that job interviewer—tries to be objective, but most interviewers *are* influenced by what they see. What do they see when you walk in the door?

Do they see you at your best? Or do they see you with your most casual take-me-as-I-am-or-don't-take-me look?

Consider this for a minute: If you're like the rest of us, you are bound to make some mistakes in your approach to job finding. Why, then, make a mistake in an area you can control—your appearance?

Sometimes there is only a hairline's difference among candidates. When that is the case, it's the neatest hairline that wins.

So it is with fresher, cleaner breath, and more conservative dress.

With all the rules and regulations governing employment, most employers won't admit to any of the reasons they refuse applicants—publicly, that is.

Privately? Privately, they'll tell you they prefer the neatly turned-out applicant, the applicant who pays the company the compliment of being sufficiently interested in the job to dress appropriately for the occasion.

And "What is appropriate dress?" you ask. Most often it's matching or coordinated colors in suit or dress. (Many employers do not like pantsuits for women.) For men, a suit is almost always preferred. The white shirt with conservative tie evokes the most favorable response.

I know of one company—no, not my former employer, though one of equal prominence—that prefers extremely conservative garb. "How conservative?" you ask. Well, if a suit has a pattern that is discernible at fifteen feet, it is too loud. As to color, blues and grays seem to be winners.

You'll probably want to ask an employee of the company concerned or your employment counselor what mode of dress is preferred.

If you're applying for a construction job, for example, you naturally are not going to wear a suit and tie, but your overall (no pun intended) appearance is important.

The healthy look is a plus. That means clean, healthy teeth and a glow of cleanliness. Sometimes a few minutes under a sunlamp can impart a healthy glow to the skin. A deep tan usually makes the potential employer wonder where you spend most of your time.

If you can afford a professionally styled haircut, by all means get it. If you can't, you may want to avail yourself of the low-cost services provided by some hairdressing schools and barber colleges. (Other low-cost services, such as those provided by dental schools and clinics, are also available.)

Your posture also affects the impression you create. Many employers think they can learn about an applicant's energy by the way he or she sits or walks.

Finally, the employer assumes you look your best. The smart applicant does.

Only when you look your best can you forget yourself enough to be yourself in the interview.

Packaging the Product: A Checklist

Here is a checklist for packaging the product you are going to sell. The product is *you.*

Since you need to be well grounded, let's start with

Shoes. Closed-toe shoes for both men and women are preferred. High-stacked heels for men are inappropriate. It's best not to be down-at-the-heel either, so do see to repairs if warranted. Use polish if your shoes require it.

Clothing. Conservative. A skirted suit or tailored dress for women. Matching jacket and trousers for men (business and professional candidates need to wear a tie and a white or light-colored shirt). For factory, construction, or similar work, wear sturdy work clothes (matching trousers and shirt will up your odds). If uniforms are necessary for the job, they are suitable for the interview.

Stockings. For women, bare legs will lower your chances of landing a job. Always wear hose or pantyhose. For men, executive-length (just below the knee), dark socks are best. If you have a foot problem and must wear white socks with a business suit, wear a dark-colored pair of socks *over* the white ones.

Jewelry. Conservative. No dangling anything—bracelets, long chains, earrings. Large rings on men cause negative reactions. More than two rings can seem too many to some interviewers.

What to Carry? A neat handbag or attaché case for women—not both. An attaché case for men if it's needed for papers.

Face and Hands. Clean-looking. Neat eyebrows enhance the well-groomed look. Even men can profit by trimming unnecessary hair from eyebrows. Also trim unsightly hair from nose and ears.

Hair. The controlled look is a winner. Long hair still costs jobs for many male candidates.

Makeup. Subtle is the look to seek.

Teeth. Clean and shiny. If you have missing teeth, try to have them replaced before you seek a job. Yes, this has cost jobs. Sometimes the interviewer thinks poor teeth signal poor health or worries that you might soon take time from the job in order to have dental work done.

Nails. Clean and well cared for. Even the auto mechanic should not advertise his trade with dirty nails.

Scent. Clean. No perfume. Only the lightest of after-shave scents or cologne, if any.

Body Language. Look alert. Sit straight. Walk with energy. Shake hands firmly. Neither a boneless nor a bone-crusher handshake is desirable.

Expression. This is probably the most important thing you wear. Make it pleasant. Many interviewers judge that always important characteristic—attitude—by your expression.

Detractions. All of the following detract from an otherwise good impression and in some instances cost a job.

- hats on male candidates (worn during the interview)
- toothpicks
- chewing gum
- nail biting
- chipped nail polish (especially dark polish)
- sunglasses worn during the interview
- glasses that are out of style
- slit skirt (this may be a cut too much)
- threads hanging from a garment
- tattoos
- bow ties

What Service Should You Offer?

To find the answer to that, some questions are in order—some questions to yourself about yourself. Take a pen and piece of paper and jot down your responses to the following questions.

About Identity

- Who am I? Forgive me, but I can't just put that bald

question at the beginning of this section without saying this: Who am I? *is* an important question but it is not the *only important* question here, so please don't become stuck on it. Actually, I give a bit more weight to this next one.

- Whose am I? To whom am I loyal? Who is important to me? To whom am I important?

About Experience

- Have I ever had a "mountaintop" experience? What was it?
- What am I particularly proud of? Is it something I've done? Or is it something I am?
- Was there a time when I was completely wrapped up in something? What was it?
- When was I happiest? What was I doing then?
- If I could use only one word to describe myself, what would that word be? Reader? Dancer? Worker? Mother? Father? Wife? Husband? Careerist? Teacher? Engineer? Optimist? Pessimist? Daughter? Son?
- What is possible for me?
- What is probable for me? What am I probably becoming if I continue on the present course?

About Environment

- Do I like small towns or big cities? Do I like to drive (enough to drive through traffic every day)? Would I like to car pool to work? Would I like to use public transportation? Is public transportation available? Would I enjoy walking to and from work?
- Do I want to work indoors or outdoors? Can I be in one location all day or must I move about?
- Do I need a stress-free environment? Or do I work best when things are popping all over?
- Do I work better at home or in an office?
- Do I like to work alone or with others? Do I like people? But, more important, am I objective about them?

About Job Structure

- Can I work well for someone else, or must I be my own boss?
- Am I a self-starter, or am I a self-rewarder? (Both are important if you want to be your own boss.)
- At what level do I want to enter an organization? Would my entry be easier at a lower level? Or must I have the stimulation of a responsible position from the outset?
- Do I lead, or am I a better follower? (There are a lot of leaders around, so some good followers are desperately needed.)

About My Preferences

- What do I enjoy doing at home?
- What community jobs do I do? Which ones do I enjoy?
- What tasks do I *dislike* doing around the house? Cooking? Yard work? Cleaning? Decorating? Child care?
- When I have free time, what do I love to do?

About Other People

- Whom do I envy? Who do I wish I were? What does that person do who is such a go-getter? What ability does he or she have that I'd like to have?
- Whom do I admire? Who are three people who are deserving of my respect? What do they have in common with each other? What do they have in common with me?
- What kind of associates do I want? Do I have any age preferences? Do I want to meet those of the opposite sex at work?

What's Important to Me?

- What do I care most about? Money? Security of job? Recognition? Power? Varied routine? Clear duties? Promotional possibilities? A chance to serve?

How Can I Serve?

- What can I do that will solve an employer's problems? Reduce the work load? Increase production? Increase profits? Reduce costs? Improve the work environment—physically? emotionally?
- What can I do to serve others?

What Excuses Do I Make to Myself About the Difficulty of Job Seeking?

Do I think I am:

- too old?
- too young?
- hurt because "all the good jobs go to Blacks"?
- hurt because I am Black, a veteran, an ex-offender?
- discriminated against because I am physically disabled, hearing-impaired, blind, or otherwise handicapped?
- overqualified?
- underqualified?
- lacking in experience?
- the victim of having taken the wrong college major?
- discriminated against because I am a woman? A man?
- in the wrong field of work?
- living in the wrong area?
- a victim of bad references?
- "out of touch" or "only a housewife"?

Please study the lists of excuses carefully. Have you ever used one of them? Now, another question: Has anyone with one of the problems listed ever landed a job? Of course. If that person can do it, so can you.

The purpose of asking yourself all these questions is to help you know yourself better.

Only when you know yourself can you know what you want to *do*.

I hope you notice how I emphasize *do*. Truly, I would put it in neon lights if possible.

Why?

Because it isn't enough to know what you want to be. When you take a job, what you do, for most of your waking hours, is of paramount importance.

This brief example explains the point better than all the philosophizing we might indulge in.

> Clarisse told me that all her life she wanted to be a doctor's assistant. Not until she became a doctor's assistant did she realize that was not the kind of work she wanted to do. "All those insurance forms and all those complaining patients to deal with. Everybody's sick. Me too. I hate it."

Keep these questions and your answers firmly in mind when you decide where you want to sell your services. In the next chapter, "The Territory," possibilities are mentioned that you've probably never before considered.

Review Questions

1. Should you ask the employer to give you a job? If yes, explain. If no, why not?
2. What is the product being sold in a job interview?
3. What can the car owner learn about the job interview from his experience in selling his car?
4. What can you do if you can't afford expensive hair care or dental care?
5. Describe an appropriate job-seeking outfit for a woman. Describe an appropriate job-seeking outfit for a man.
6. Will the interviewer usually explain a turndown to the candidate?
7. (True or False) If your paycheck is small, it doesn't add much to the company's costs. Explain.
8. Are there enough jobs available so that the average job seeker can find one?

CHAPTER 2

The Territory

How to Organize a Prospect File

In the opening scene of the musical *The Music Man,* a group of salesmen discuss their work. To the beat of the music, they chant over and over, "You can talk, you can talk, but you gotta know the territory." They are right. *You gotta know the territory* if you're going to sell the product.

The product we're talking about is you. The territory is the area where you conduct your job search.

By culling information about prospective employers in your territory, you develop your prospect file. A good salesperson has a card on every prospect.

You can design that card in a number of ways. But you must make one for *every prospect on your list.* A three-by-five-inch index card is all you need. You may use my format if you wish; I use both sides of the card, as shown here.

Prospect Card

Name of Organization: ....
(check spelling)
Type of Business:..
Interviewer's name: M. ....
Interviewer's title, if any: ....
Date & time of interview:.....................................
Company address:..
Is there more than one location?............................
Telephone:.................... Hours of work: ....
Name of friends in the organization:.......................
....
Result of interview: ☐ Are they to call? ☐ Am I to call?
When?...... When?.......
Names of others I met: ....
....

Prospect Card (Reverse Side)

Checklist—Prospect Follow-up

The following factors are vital to the outcome of every job interview. Ask yourself the following questions:

1. Have I expressed positive interest in the job? Does the employer know I want to work for the organization?
2. Have I sent a follow-up note of thanks? This is not a mere courtesy; it serves as a reminder to the interviewer.
3. If rejected for the job discussed, have I asked to be considered for future openings? If the rejection is total, have I asked the interviewer to tell me how to strengthen my next interviews?
4. Have I asked the interviewer for referrals to other employers? This is probably the most important step in any job search. Personnel people know who's hiring. What's more, they like to help the candidate they've had to reject.

How to Discover Where the Jobs Are

You will need to ply every one of the sources I've gathered here, as well as a few of your own, in order to make the best possible list of prospective employers. Remember, it usually takes twenty interviews to net five solid job offers.

Friends. You'll notice I put friends at the top of this list. I assure you that's where they belong. A large chunk of applicants, about 30 to 40 percent, find jobs through this one source.

While I consider all friends a part of your network, I put their referrals in two categories:

1. The polite referral. This one gets you off their backs

but not onto anyone's payroll. It's usually the outcome of a poor-me-I-don't-know-where-to-look request.

2. The solid lead to a job or person in an organization who has the power to create a job. Cultivate this second kind. This one is the outcome of a friend's realization that you have something to offer.

Friends who are looking for jobs themselves can be a great source of help for *you.* There are many good reasons for this. Because you're rarely alike in qualifications and interests, you can exchange leads you don't need, and you can exchange up-to-the-minute news and campaign tips. Also, the psychological benefits of this mutual exchange are enormous. You not only act as a spur for each other, but also you can commiserate with each other over rejection. For when a friend you admire experiences rejection, you begin to realize you are not alone in the experience. *Everybody* who is out there trying is going to be rejected—a lot of the time. This helps you to say "so what" and try again.

If there is a job-seekers club or group in your area, join it. Job Seekers Anonymous, which is usually open to anyone who is honestly trying to find work, and Forty-Plus Club, which is a group of executive job seekers who are over forty years of age, are two such groups.

Libraries. Make use of every library to which you have access or can gain access.

The Public Library. Every job seeker is invited to use the services and resources of the public library. Look in the business and careers sections. Consult any newspapers that have pertinent information. Also ask to see *Forbes* magazine, *Fortune* magazine, *Dun and Bradstreet Directory, Standard & Poor's Register of Corporations, Directories and Executives,* and the *Occupational Outlook Handbook* (the current one—this is updated every two years). While you're at the public library, ask if they have a directory of special libraries and information centers for your area. Librarians—bless them all—want to help, and do. Some of them will probably tell you how to gain access to special libraries.

Special Libraries.

- *Professional.* Doctors, lawyers, engineers, and many other professionals maintain their own libraries.
- *Educational Institutions.* Almost every university and school has a library.
- *Business.* These include company libraries as well as libraries in brokerage houses and other similar organizations.

I've just mentioned a few places that have libraries and information centers. There are many more. Some are tucked away in churches, YMCAs, YWCAs, and other organizations. Ask around.

School Placement Offices. These include high schools, business schools, and universities. While you're at the school, check the alumni office. Also, talk with teachers and fellow students as well as with fraternity and sorority associates. Your success in the job world reflects favorably on your school. They want to help, and it doesn't matter to most schools whether you were a student last year or ten years ago. If they have helpful information, they're eager to part with it.

Telephone Directories. There is a quick-reference index in almost all telephone directories. In the larger cities this index is usually placed at the beginning of the Yellow Pages. It is an idea gold mine. Every single time I pick up one of these I find listings of businesses I'd never heard of previously. Try it.

Government and Social Services. Go back to your trusty phone directory. There you will find listings of all government and social service agencies. But you haven't looked thoroughly until you have looked under each listing—city, county, state, and U.S. governments.

Telephone state, county, and municipal offices for information about when and where examinations will be held. Ask about any special procedures.

If you need help in sorting out federal agencies (who doesn't?), look for the number of the Federal Information Center in your area. It's a hotline. The person answering should be able to direct you to any person or bureau within the U.S. government. This number usually appears under the heading "U.S. Government," and it is almost always in the White Pages.

Post Office. Always check the post office bulletin board for the most current information about civil service jobs.

Chambers of Commerce. Your chamber should have a complete list of all the companies in your area. Some will even have listings of executives as well. And some will be able to tell you about companies that are moving to the area.

If your town is too small to have its own chamber of commerce, try the state chamber of commerce.

Newspapers. Study all of them, including the weeklies. Read *every* issue of the local papers and as many as possible of the business newspapers. *(The Wall Street Journal, The New York Times,* etc.). Don't just read the want ads but also read the articles about businesses that reach the front page as well as the business section. This is how you find out about mergers, expansions, and executive promotions. This is how you get the name of the *live person* in the company to whom you address your letter of application, or whom you telephone. (It can be a real help to have seen the picture of your interviewer in a news release. This saves your wondering if every person you pass on the way to your appointment is "the one.")

Your Own Ad. This is not the best source of prospects, but is *one* way. You might want to consider a trade journal for this as well as a newspaper.

Observations. Learn to observe. Don't just join the gaping sidewalk superintendents when you see a new building going up. Ask yourself, "Will this new apartment building need a new manager?" "Who is going to staff this huge new office building?" "Who is going to manage this new book store?" "Will this new restaurant need workers?"

Trade, Professional, and Civic Meetings. Attend all meetings where the movers and shakers congregate. Ask for advice and referrals.

Betty Hudson, Vice-President of Corporate Relations for the National Broadcasting Company, said that the best boost she ever gave her own career was attendance at a conference of television personnel in Denver. (She went at her own expense.)

Former Employers. Ask all former employers for their advice and referrals. These people are surprisingly helpful. I could never have become a Procter & Gamble retread without the help of Walter Emmerling, my former boss.

Service Organizations. Altrusa International, B'nai B'rith, National Exchange Club, Kiwanis International, Rotary International, YMCA, YWCA, Business and Professional Women's Club, and other service organizations can provide help. They sponsor special workshops and job-seeking seminars. You will also want to check the Catalyst National Roster, if appropriate (this organization provides services for college-trained women; their materials are excellent and current).

Boards of Education. Each municipality has its own board of education, and you have not really applied for a job in the field of education until you have looked under each listing. Don't forget private, special interest, and commercial schools.

Employment Agencies. *Public.* Each state has its own bureau of employment services. Look for the one nearest you. This service is free. Some of the larger bureaus provide a testing service also. And did you know that every company that holds a government contract is required by law to list its openings with the state bureau of employment?

Private. Every time I'm asked what I think of buy-a-jobs or commercial agencies, I hem and haw a lot. Some are good. Some are just horrible. How can you tell? As a start, find out how long your employment counselor has been in the field. The good ones welcome the question. You may also ask whether or not any of the client companies pay them. Usually, a company will not become a client unless they get ethical service. Notice I talk about the company getting the service; you see, the job of the agency is finding people for jobs and not jobs for people. There is this to be said for the experience of going to a commercial agency counselor: That counselor will usually level with you in a way that the company representative cannot. If your appearance is rotten or your attitude poor, they usually tell you.

Temporary Work. There is no easier way to enter or reenter the work force than by doing temporary work. The simplest way to do this is to register with an employment contractor. (You usually find "Employment Contractors" under that heading in the Yellow Pages.) Do notice I said contractor, not agency. The employment contractors are the ones who hold the contracts with employers for temporary assignments. This area of work has grown much more sophisticated in recent years. Why? Because many employers don't want to fool around with all those records and pay all those benefits (particularly Workmen's Compensation).

Temporary employment is the coming trend. In the 1980s you'll see a great many people, in all fields and specialties, so employed. Think about it.

The U.S. government is beginning to set about making a large percentage of government jobs temporary. Others will follow.

Your Elected Officials. Take advantage of any help provided by your mayor's office, by your district and state representatives' offices, by your governor's office, and by your senators' offices. Somebody who is up for reelection will want to help you. Ask, "How can your office help me?"

and "What new agencies or foundations can provide help for me?"

If you are a veteran, be sure to add the Veterans Administration to this list. They have placement specialists on the staff. You'll also want to ask about the extra points veterans are given on civil service (and some municipal) exams.

Work for Yourself. If you have a unique service or product to offer and if you can sell yourself, this can be a very good idea. If you do decide to start your own business, call those helpful people at SCORE (Service Corps of Retired Executives). This is a volunteer group, and you track them down through the Small Business Administration office closest to you. You find the listing under U.S. government in the White Pages of your telephone directory.

Review Questions

1. Name three prospect sources.
2. How do you develop a prospect list?
3. What does the chamber of commerce do? How can the chamber be of help to the job seeker?
4. What is the difference between a public employment bureau and a private employment agency?
5. (True or False) It is important to know what the company makes or does.
6. Name two kinds of libraries.
7. (True or False) Once you graduate or leave your school, it is no longer interested in your job search.
8. (True or False) Almost all job openings are listed in the want ads.
9. (True or False) Former employers can be helpful in your job search.
10. Make a list of twenty prospective employers.

CHAPTER 3

The Tools of the Job-Hunting Trade

The Letter of Application

Few candidates for a position are hired without an interview. Therefore, you must first concentrate on the most effective way to obtain an interview.

By all accounts, the letter of application is the best way.

In developing an effective letter of application, you must remember this above all else: You're asking for an interview, *not for a job.* That comes later. First things first, and the first order of business is to attract the attention of the employer, in a positive way and in an original way.

It's so tempting and comforting to copy a *typical* letter of application, insert the employer's name, and send it off. That's not the way it works. You need an *atypical* letter, one that expresses *you.*

You'll want to start with an attention getter, what we in the newspaper business call a news peg or hook—something that will catch the eye and interest of the person with the power to hire you. This news peg or hook is there if you'll look for it. Ask yourself, "What attracted me to this company or field of work?" An outstanding story on the business pages? A remark by a friend? A speech I heard by one of its officers? Whatever it is, use it.

Look over my shoulder a minute and see what one of my readers wrote to me: "Apparently there's something wrong with my letter of application. I sent out one hundred letters over a month ago. So far I've had two answers, and neither was encouraging. In fact, they were downright discouraging. Can you help?"

Here's what I said to Dejected and Rejected: "Yes, I can help. You can help even more by asking yourself several important questions.

1. Did you send the same letter to all those companies?
2. Was your letter one that could have come from someone else, or was it a letter that was uniquely yours?
3. Was it addressed to a company or to a particular person in that company? Did you spell the name correctly? Are you sure?
4. Did you say you hoped to hear from them, or words to that effect?
5. Did you sign the letter? Did you include your address and phone number?
6. Did you have someone you trust look it over for errors?"

Answer these questions honestly and check the following guidelines. Let me assure you the following points reflect advice from many personnel interviewers (more than I can count or have the space to name here). My tips are woven in, too.

Guidelines

- The guiding principle is this: Be specific. Your letter should be so specific that no one else could possibly have written it. Your letter should be so specific that it could go to no other person, save the one addressed.
- Let the follow-up be with you, the seller. You're selling your services, remember? *You* retain control over suggesting and setting up an appointment time. You won't have to wait around for them to call or write. You will be flexible, of course.
- Learn the correct name of the company and of the company representative. Spell those names correctly. Elementary? Yes. Generally observed? No. The personnel people at J. C. Penn*e*y Company, Inc., are

nodding in agreement. So are those at Emery Industries, Inc., and at The Procter & Gamble Company.

- Write to a specific person, not just to a company.
- Your letter should be neatly typed on standard 8½-by-11-inch white or light paper.
- Have someone you trust look over your letter to point out any errors in spelling or in grammar.
- Put your name and address on the letter and on the envelope. If the interviewer or employer can't get in touch with you, you won't get many job offers. Also, it's common office etiquette to sign all letters.
- The prospective employer expects an original letter from you. While it is acceptable to duplicate or print your résumé, provided you do it well, it is not good practice to send a form letter of application. Form letters beget form letters. If you send one, the odds are ten-to-one you'll receive one in reply.
- Avoid flattery, exaggerated expressions of gratitude, and begging.
- Don't brag. Self-appraisal is fine. Self-praise kills the sale.

The perfect letter of application is still to be written. I'm convinced of that. Having read tens of thousands of the blamed things, I decided to take a shot at writing one, and to let it serve as your example.

I'm embarrassed to tell you how long I slaved over my letter. So I won't. I will say this: I followed the guidelines I've worked so hard to establish. Take a look at my letter, and then go back over the guidelines.

First, let me tell you how I selected the recipient of my letter. My husband came home one balmy spring evening and told me he was swamped with letters of application from senior chemistry and chemical engineering students and didn't need any more candidates. I said nothing to him but set to work on this letter early the next morning:

C.P.O. 1190
Wheaton, Illinois 60187
(312) 000-0000

April 17, 19—

Dr. J. Bruce Martin
The Procter & Gamble Company
Ivorydale Technical Center
June Street and Spring Grove Avenue
Cincinnati, Ohio 45217

Dear Dr. Martin:

Five years ago you awakened my interest in The Procter & Gamble Company. You were a judge at the Engineering Society's Science Awards Exhibit. I was a contestant in the chemistry classification.

Much has changed since then, but not my interest in chemistry nor my interest in Procter & Gamble.

In June of this year I will graduate with a B.S. in chemistry from Wheaton College. Since I plan to be in Cincinnati in late May, I should like very much to talk with you again (or with someone on your staff).

I will telephone your office long distance early next week to arrange an interview date.

Sincerely,

David P. Post

P.S. There is no reason you should remember this as well as I do—I was a second-place winner in a field of eighty-seven.

The kind of information I used in the letter to Dr. Martin is available to anyone who reads newspapers. Both our metropolitan dailies carried news of the Science Awards Exhibits, including names of judges and exhibitors.

When my husband, Bruce, said he planned to telephone

the candidate, I had to confess to writing the letter.

We're speaking again, and he has been decent about the whole incident—and has even helped me proofread this text.

Here are two more examples of letters of application. Both of them won interviews—and ultimately jobs—for the senders. I did not use real names, just real letters.

603 Mountain View Ridge
Waynesboro, Virginia 22980
(702) 000-0000

February 28, 19—

Skyler H. Robinson
Vice-President
Foster Chemicals
Center and Main Streets
Waynesboro, Virginia 22980

Dear Mr. Robinson:

My attendance at the seventy-fifth anniversary celebration of your company last month was in response to the casual invitation of a friend. But there is nothing casual about this letter.

The remarks you made on that occasion so intrigued me that I made a point of learning more about Foster Chemicals. I'd like to learn still more.

I'm confident you would find a personal meeting interesting; it could prove mutually profitable as well. I say this because some of my experience in the chemical marketing research field relates to what you are doing and apparently plan to do at Foster Chemicals.

I will telephone your secretary in a few days to arrange an interview or brief talk at your convenience.

Sincerely,

Carolyn E. Rodgers

10654 Doepke Court
Chicago, Illinois 60637
(312) 000-0000

May 14, 19—

P. O. Box 124
℅ *The Chicago-Sun Times*
401 North Wabash Avenue
Chicago, Illinois 60611

Dear Employer:

The position you describe briefly in today's *Chicago-Sun Times* is intriguing to me. The "background in sales and advertising" you mention is a requirement I meet.

As part of my school's cooperative education program, I sold better sportswear for Rodgers Fashion Department Store. In recognition of my receiving a special award for volume of sales, I was permitted to work under Lacey Lasky in the advertising section during the last quarter of the cooperative period.

I would appreciate an opportunity to discuss the advertised opening with you as well as any other you anticipate having in the next month or so.

Enclosed is a copy of the résumé you requested. I look forward to meeting you personally.

Sincerely yours,

Dabney E. Martin, Jr.

As you see, this letter was sent in response to a blind ad. The ad asked for a résumé but said nothing about a covering letter. Although the candidate who sent this letter was not the only one interviewed, he was the only one who sent a letter. He was told that he would not have been invited for an interview on the basis of the résumé alone because his age (twenty-two) was against him.

The Résumé

Reprinted by permission. © 1979 NEA, Inc.

Your résumé. You pronounce it ray′-zoo-may or rez′-oo-may. (I checked three dictionaries and could not get complete agreement.) All the authorities make it three syllables.

Or, if saying résumé makes you nervous, refer to it as a data sheet.

What is a résumé?

It's a condensed career autobiography. It's *you* on one white or light 8½-by-11-inch piece of quality paper (at most, two 8½-by-11-inch pieces of paper). Take heart, if they can get the Gettysburg Address on the head of a pin, surely you can describe yourself in a page or two.

Why bother with a résumé?

Because most employers expect one. Because it clarifies your thinking. Even if you *never* show it to anyone, it will help you to present yourself better.

Your mind is like a computer. It will store the information you place there. If you store your job information in an organized way, it will flow out of you in an organized way.

What kind of résumé is best?

You'll want to consider what is easiest for you. There are three basic designs:

1. The chronological résumé. This is a factual record of the jobs you've held and the schools you've attended, all in chronological order.

2. The functional résumé. This design lets you tell not only where you worked but what you did there—your accomplishments. Specific examples are best. You might talk about:
   - any unusual responsibility you carried out
   - how you helped the company grow
   - how you saved the company money
   - your rapid promotions
   - your demonstrated leadership

   And you might include a comment made about you or written to you. But don't put *all* these things in. These examples are merely to spark your thoughts. What you include will be different because you're different.
3. The original-idea résumé. Often this turns out to be too gimmicky and of a size and shape that makes it difficult to keep.

Pointers for a Winning Résumé—What's Included? Certainly not all of you but the best of you. Don't offer the whole hog. Trim off the undesirable parts and offer the most edible. Do not include any information that might serve to eliminate you. This could be height, weight, sex, age, number of children, educational limitations, marital status, or physical handicaps. Remember, you are writing a promotional piece. You are not to tell everything you know about yourself.

Consolidate. Tie similar experiences together. Use headings.

Keep it short. The employer is going to speed read your résumé. Be sure it lends itself to this. One page is usually sufficient.

Purpose. A résumé is used as bait. It's to trigger the desire of the potential employer to learn more about you. It does not have to be thorough to do this. Ask yourself this question, "Does my résumé shape my experience to fit the job I'm seeking?"

Suggestion: If you are interested in several fields of work, make several sets of résumés. That way, your job objective can be clear-cut on each set. Try to use the same words in the job title that your prospective employer uses.

Checklist. Be Sure to Include:

1. Your name.
2. Your address. Don't laugh. I'd estimate that at least 10 percent of job applicants forget their name or address.
3. Your phone number. You double your chances for a call if you also leave a number where a message can be taken for you.
4. Your job objective.
5. Highlights of your education.
6. Highlights of your work experience (include work for which you were not paid if it strengthens your case). Don't just tell what you did, tell *how* you did it.
7. Date of availability.
8. Any other qualification that makes you a superior candidate for a particular job.

When Should a Résumé Be Used? Some very astute personnel counselors say, "Make a résumé but don't send it with your letter of application. Save it for the follow-up letter after the interview." I say use it when *you* think it will do the most for you. You might want to:

- include it with your letter of application to strengthen the letter
- leave it with the interviewer. A résumé can be very effective in talking for you if the interviewer reviews your file with someone else or if the interview has been cut short due to an unforeseen circumstance. (There have been occasions when I didn't want to waste applicant time with application forms because I couldn't foresee a suitable opening. You guessed it: The unforeseen developed, and the résumés gave me the needed information.)
- enclose it with the follow-up letter you will write.

How About Professionally Crafted Résumés? Professionally crafted résumés are attractive. They are always carefully typed (a must for any résumé). The duplicating equipment used is almost always in excellent condition.

But here are the dangers: If the potential employer recognizes your résumé as a professionally crafted one, you lose. Instead of being impressed, the employer wonders about your initiative and your ability to communicate. You can also lose the advantage of having thought about what it is you have to offer; so you find yourself mouthing someone else's words in the interview. When someone else's words come out of you, those words sound very stilted.

There is no such thing as the perfect résumé. Just do your best and get on with the job hunt.

Sample Résumés. Either of the following résumé designs will work well for the average candidate. Obviously the design of the simplified résumé makes this one easier to construct. However, if you've had some unusual work experiences, you might use the format of the functional résumé.

Outline for Simplified Résumé

NAME: Smith, John David

ADDRESS: 606 Main Street, Big City, Maine 04330

TELEPHONE: (207) 000-0000
Message can be taken at (207) 000-1111

JOB OBJECTIVE: If you're familiar with the employer's terminology, use it.

EDUCATION:

WORK EXPERIENCE:

Whichever of these two categories is the more impressive should be listed directly under the job objective.

If you hold a degree, you won't need to waste space on high school background; unless, of course, you were valedictorian or class president.

SPECIAL SKILLS/ATTRIBUTES:

This is the section where your résumé should be different. Think about the job requirements and list those skills/attributes that show how you meet them.

Each item mentioned here won a job interview for the person who listed it:

- knowledge of a foreign language (tell which one)
- knowledge of sign language
- knowledge of procedures for federal grant requests
- knowledge of a computer language (tell which one)
- ability to type sixty words per minute
- knowledge of shorthand
- knowledge of CPR (cardiopulmonary resuscitation)
- ability to handle ⅔-axle vehicles
- willing to travel or relocate
- have own transportation (One young man mentioned five years of accident-free driving and won a job.)

REFERENCES: If you decide to use them, be sure you include full addresses and phone numbers. Also, indicate that you have the permission of the person listed.

NOTE: The candidates I work with are outstandingly successful when they attach a letter of reference instead of listing references. My guess is that the employer responds favorably because this practice saves so much work for him or her.

Outline for Functional Résumé

Shirlie Jane Doe

24 Mockingbird Terrace Cincinnati, Ohio 45331	Single—willing to travel and relocate
Telephone: (513) 000-0000 or leave message 000-0000	Available immediately
JOB OBJECTIVE:	Field of personnel (selection and recruitment nontechnical personnel)

WORK EXPERIENCE:

July 25, 1964 to April 1, 1981	The Pyramid Manufacturing Company 1234 XYZ Street Finneytown Hill, Cincinnati, Ohio 45201

Selected personnel for executive offices. Developed a training-grant program to guarantee an inflow of competent secretaries. Cost saving of $15,000 the first six months, increased savings thereafter.

Worked with our public relations department and local press on series of articles about our employees. Result: A sharp drop in turnover and an equally sharp rise in the number of job candidates. We ran no want ads during this period. Money saved from the advertising budget was used to implement the program mentioned above.

June 25, 1958 to July 25, 1964	Acme Temporary Placements 5678 ABC Street Cincinnati, Ohio 45201

Client sales. One of my clients was Pyramid. They negotiated with my employer when an opening developed in their personnel department.

EDUCATION:	Walnut Hills High School, graduated 1954 University of Cincinnati, 1954-1956 University of Miami, Coral Gables, Florida, 1956-1958 (B.A. in English) University of Cincinnati Evening College (personnel courses including tests and measurements, techniques of interviewing, and communications)

Important Numbers, Cards, and Papers

When you're job hunting, it's a good idea to have the following items handy:

- social security card
- all correspondence between you and the prospective employer
- union card
- grade transcripts
- sample certification card for registered nurse, engineer, etc.
- health certificate
- military discharge papers

The Application Form

Many employers will ask that you fill out an application form. Are there special tricks to filling out an application form? Indeed, yes. If you follow the six tips given here, your application will work for you, not against you as so many do.

- Fill out a master application form and carry it with you when you look for a job. I have provided various sample forms on pages 41–49. Be sure to include full names where indicated and use complete addresses. By using the master form, it will be easier for you to fill out the actual form. It will also make you seem more professional if you're required to fill out an employer's application form on the premises. You won't be one of those ill-prepared candidates who has to borrow the receptionist's phone directory.
- If at all possible, ask to fill out the application form at home. This gives you a chance to duplicate the form. Of course, you'll fill out the copy first. This practice will make the original form look much neater, for you'll have a chance to see how your answers look in all those little spaces. Also, you'll have a permanent copy of what you wrote.
- List a second phone number where a message can be taken for you. This can double your chances for that all-important call.

- Sign the application form. Many employers do not consider an application valid unless it has a signature.
- Fill in every space. If the question doesn't seem to pertain to you, draw a line to show that you saw the question. If an unfair question is asked, about age, for example, merely put N/A (not applicable).
- If at all possible, type the application form. A typed application form evokes the most positive response from the employer. If you must complete the application form at the employment office, use *your* pen, not theirs. Employment office pens are worse than those you find in post offices. Use a pen with black ink (no fancy colors such as green or purple).

Let me tell you about a bit of research I did on your behalf. It came about because I said to myself, "If John T. Molloy considers reaction to color so important in clothing, perhaps there is an important reaction to the color of ink used in filling out application forms."

There is! I made up a test that examined ink-color preferences. In order to make a fair test, I had the same persons fill out the forms using the various colors of ink. I asked employment managers to tell me which candidates they would invite in for interview "based only on the appearance of the application form."

I am surprised at my own findings. The most significant one: The reaction to application forms filled out in black ink is much more positive than the reaction to those filled out in any other color—even blue. Here are some of my other findings:

- The typed application form ranks first.
- The one filled out in black ink ranks second.
- Midnight blue ink was a poor third.
- Medium blue was next, but it was not even close to midnight blue or black.
- Brown ink followed medium blue.
- Greens, purples, and other colors produced a negative reaction.

Application For Employment

(answer all questions - please print)

In compliance with Federal and State equal employment opportunity laws, qualified applicants are considered for all positions without regard to race, color, religion, sex, national origin, age, marital status, or the presence of a non-job-related medical condition or handicap.

Date of Application__________

Position(s) Applied For __________

Referral Source ☐ Advertisement ☐ Friend ☐ Relative

☐ Employment Agency ☐ Other__________

Name __________ LAST FIRST MIDDLE Social Security No.__________

Address __________ CITY STATE ZIP Phone No. __________

Are you known to schools/references by another name? ☐ Yes ☐ No

If yes, by what name? __________

Have you filed an application or been employed here before? ☐ Yes ☐ No Date(s) __________

Are you a Citizen of the United States? ☐ Yes ☐ No

If not, do you possess an Alien Registration Card? ☐ Yes ☐ No

Are you available to work? ☐ Full Time ☐ Part Time ☐ On Shifts

Do Any of Your Friends or Relatives Work Here? ☐ Yes ☐ No

If Yes, List Name(s) __________

Are you? ☐ Under 18 ☐ 18-70 ☐ Over 70 years of age

Have you been convicted of a felony or released from prison within the last 7 years? ☐ Yes ☐ No

If yes, describe in full, including date(s)__________

In case of accident or emergency, please notify:

NAME ADDRESS PHONE NO.

AN EQUAL EMPLOYMENT OPPORTUNITY EMPLOYER M/F

Are You On Lay-Off And Subject To Recall? ☐ Yes ☐ No

What Foreign Languages Do You Speak, Read, and/or Write Fluently?

	GOOD	FAIR	POOR
SPEAK			
READ			
WRITE			

Can You Travel If A Job Requires It? ☐ Yes ☐ No

Have You Been Bonded? ☐ Yes ☐ No

If Yes, For Which Position(s) ____________________

Do You Have A Disability, A Handicap or A Medical Condition That Limits Your Job Performance? ☐ Yes ☐ No

If Yes, Please Explain ____________________

____

____

____

Are You A Veteran? ☐ Yes ☐ No

If Yes, What Was Your Branch of Military Service? ____________________ Rank ________

List Trade or Professional Organizations Of Which You Are A Member, Including Offices Held

____

____

____

Give Name, Address and Phone Number Of Three References Not Related To You

____

____

____

Employment Experience

List each job held. Start with your Present or Last job. Include military service assignments and volunteer activities.

		Dates		Work Performed
1	Employer	From	To	
	Address			
	Job Title	Hrly. Rate/Salary		
		Starting	Final	
	Supervisor			
	Reason for Leaving			
		Dates		Work Performed
2	Employer	From	To	
	Address			
	Job Title	Hrly. Rate/Salary		
		Starting	Final	
	Supervisor			
	Reason for Leaving			
		Dates		Work Performed
3	Employer	From	To	
	Address			
	Job Title	Hrly. Rate/Salary		
		Starting	Final	
	Supervisor			
	Reason for Leaving			
		Dates		Work Performed
4	Employer	From	To	
	Address			
	Job Title	Hrly. Rate/Salary		
		Starting	Final	
	Supervisor			
	Reason for Leaving			

If you need additional space, please continue on a separate sheet of paper.

Summarize Special Skills and Qualifications
Acquired From Employment Or Other Experience ____________________

____

____

____

Education

	Elementary	High	College/University	Graduate/ Professional
School Name				
Years Completed: (Circle)	4 5 6 7 8	9 10 11 12	1 2 3 4	1 2 3 4
Diploma/Degree				
Describe Course Of Study:				
Describe Specialized Training, Apprenticeship, Skills, and Extra-Curricular Activities				

Agreement

I certify that answers given herein are true and complete to the best of my knowledge.

I authorize you to make such investigations and inquiries of my personal, employment, financial or medical history and other related matters as may be necessary in arriving at an employment decision. I hereby release employers, schools or persons from all liability in responding to inquiries in connection with my application.

In the event of employment, I understand that false or misleading information given in my application or interview(s) may result in discharge. I understand, also, that I am required to abide by all rules and regulations of the Company.

Signature of Applicant ____________ Date ____________

For Personnel Department Use Only

Arrange Interview ☐ Yes ☐ No Date____________

Remarks____________

Employed ☐ Yes ☐ No Date of Employment____________

Job Title ____________ Hourly Rate/Salary____________ Department____________

MASTER APPLICATION

PERSONAL DATA

NAME LAST FIRST MIDDLE	DATE AVAILABLE	FOREIGN LANGUAGES
HOME ADDRESS (Street, City, State, Zip)	HOME PHONE	U.S. CITIZEN ☐ YES ☐ NO
COLLEGE ADDRESS (Street, City, State, Zip)	COLLEGE PHONE	IF "NO" TYPE OF VISA

TYPE OF WORK

TYPE OF EMPLOYMENT DESIRED (1st. Choice)	(2nd. Choice)
WORK LOCATION RESTRICTIONS (If Any)	

EDUCATIONAL INFORMATION

NAME AND LOCATION OF SCHOOLS ATTENDED	DATES From	DATES To	DEGREE EARNED	GRADUATION DATE	MAJOR	MINOR	GRADE PT. AVERAGE (1) Overall (2) Major	GRADE BASIS	CLASS RANK QUARTILE
							1 2	A =	
							1 2	A =	
							1 2	A =	

COLLEGE HONORS, PROFESSIONAL SOCIETIES, FRATERNITIES, AND ACTIVITIES (Give Positions Held)

% COLLEGE EXPENSES EARNED	HOW EARNED

EMPLOYMENT INFORMATION

SIGNIFICANT WORK AND MILITARY EXPERIENCE (Names and Addresses of Employers)	DESCRIPTION OF WORK	HOURS PER WEEK	DATES EMPLOYED FROM	DATES EMPLOYED TO

GENERAL INFORMATION

REFERENCES (Names and Addresses — Preferably Faculty and Employers)

OTHER INFORMATION (Community Activities, Hobbies, Interests, Etc.)

SIGNATURE	DATE SIGNED

SAMPLE JOB APPLICATION FORM

To be used either to:
1. Help you to make a choice of jobs
2. To take with you on job interviews, so you can quickly copy information from this worksheet onto the employer's job application.

Name ______________________________ Social Security Number ______________
Last First Middle

Present address ______________________________

City ______________ State ______ Telephone ______________

Last previous address ______________ How long have you lived at present address? ______

For what position(s) are you applying? ______________________________

Have you had any serious illness, injury or surgery in past five years? ______ Explain: ______________

Do you have any physical disability? ______ Explain: ______________

Have you any "sideline" business interest? ______ If so, explain: ______________

Have you ever been convicted of a crime? ______ Explain: ______________

In case of accident, notify ______________ Name ______ Relationship

______________ Address ______ Telephone

EDUCATION AND TRAINING

	Name and Location of School	Years Attended	Course of Study	Date Left	Did You Graduate?
Grade School					
High School					
College or Vocational School					

List any special training or experience you have: ______________________________

____

MILITARY RECORD

Have you ever served in the armed services of the United States? ______ Which branch? ______________ Rank ______

Date entered ______ Date released ______ Reason for release ______________

Type of duties performed ______________________________

Do you have any reserve or national guard obligations? Explain: ______________

Military training schools attended ______________________________

AN EQUAL OPPORTUNITY EMPLOYER M/F

EMPLOYMENT APPLICATION

IMPORTANT - VARIOUS FEDERAL AND STATE LAWS PROHIBIT DISCRIMINATION BECAUSE OF AGE, SEX, RACE, COLOR, RELIGIOUS CREED, NATIONAL ORIGIN, ANCESTRY, PHYSICAL HANDICAP OR MILITARY STATUS. INQUIRIES AS TO AGE ARE MADE IN GOOD FAITH FOR NON-DISCRIMINATORY PURPOSES. IN COMPLETING THE APPLICATION FORM, PLEASE EXCLUDE ANY INFORMATION THE CHARACTER OF WHICH INDICATES THE RACE, COLOR, RELIGIOUS CREED, NATIONAL ORIGIN OR ANCESTRY OF THE APPLICANT. PERSONS EMPLOYED BY THIS AGENCY MAY BE REQUIRED TO PROVIDE VERIFICATION OF INFORMATION REPORTED ON THIS FORM.

ANSWER ALL APPLICABLE QUESTIONS

PERSONAL DATA

Please Print

Name	Last	First	Middle	Social Security No.
Present Address	No. Street	City State	Zip Code	Home Telephone No. ( )
Permanent Address	No. Street	City State	Zip Code	Business Telephone No. ( )
Have you ever changed your name other than by court ☐ yes ☐ no	If "Yes" State Previous Name(s) Last			
Are You A Citizen of the United States ☐ yes ☐ no	If "no" What Type Of Visa Do You Have? Expiration Date Of Visa			Date Available For Work Mo. Day
POSITION APPLIED FOR				

EDUCATION

School	Location	Dates Attended From	To	Did you Graduate? Yes	No	Course of Study

SKILLS

Skills

- /_/ Typing ______________ WPM
- /_/ Shorthand ____________ WPM
- /_/ Dictating Equipment

Other Office Or Trade Skills

Dates Employed	Name/Address of Company	Name of Supervisor	Your Position	Salary	Reason For Leaving
From				Starting	
To				Final	
From				Starting	
To				Final	
From				Starting	
To				Final	
From				Starting	
To				Final	
From				Starting	
To				Final	

HEALTH INFORMATION

Do You Have Any Physical Limitations?

/_/ yes /_/ no

If "Yes" Describe

Have You Lost Any Time From School Or Work In The Last 5 Years? (Week or More)

/_/ yes /_/ no

If "Yes" Give Details	Dates	Time Lost	Reason

Have You Ever Sought Compensation For Any Work-Related Illiness Or Injury?

/_/ yes /_/ no

If "Yes" Give Details	Dates	Time Lost	Reason

MISCELLANEOUS

Have You Ever Been Convicted Of Any Crime Other Than A Minor Traffic Offense?	If "Yes" Give Details	Dates	Court	Nature of Crime
/_/ yes /_/ no				

Branch of U.S. Military Service	Date Entered	Date Discharged	Type of Discharge

IN CASE OF EMERGENCY, PLEASE NOTIFY

Name	Address	Telephone No.

I hereby certify that all the information contained on this Application for Employment is true and complete. I authorize the Agency to contact all sources necessary to verify this information. I understand that any misstatement or omission is cause for dismissal should I be employed. I also understand that classification as a regular employee depends upon my successfully completing a probationary period.

Should I be employed by the Agency I hereby agree, in consideration of that employment, to disclose fully and assign to the Agency all inventions I conceive, make, or reduce to practice, alone or in combination with others, during my period of employment by the Agency and for a reasonable time thereafter, whether during or outside of working hours, which relate to the business of the Agency or result from tasks assigned me by the Agency, and to assist the Agency at any time during and subsequent to my employment by it, in every lawful, proper and reasonable manner, to obtain, maintain and enforce patents on said invention including the execution and assignment of all documents necessary thereto. I further agree to keep confidential, and not to use or divulge unless authorized to do so by the Agency, all confidential information and trade secrets I obtain as a result of my employment.

Signature of Applicant	Date

Review Questions

The Letter of Application

1. To whom should the letter of application be sent?
2. (True or False) It is all right to duplicate a letter of application.
3. (True or False) It is not necessary to type a letter of application.
4. (True or False) It is all right to send the same letter to several companies.
5. What kind of paper should be used?
6. Where does your name belong? On the letter? On the envelope?
7. (True or False) Responsibility for the follow-up is with the sender of the letter.
8. (True or False) The letter of application is your sales flyer.
9. (True or False) It's a good idea to look for a sample letter of application and to copy it.
10. What are the characteristics of a good letter of application? Name at least two of them.

The Résumé

1. What is a résumé?
2. Why should a job seeker make a résumé?
3. How many pages should a résumé be?
4. What type of paper should be used?
5. Is it necessary that each résumé be individually typed?
6. Should a résumé be used with the letter of application, at the time of the interview, or after the interview?
7. What are the most important items to include in a résumé? Name at least four of them.

8. What do these words mean?
   functional
   chronological
9. What are the advantages of using a professionally crafted résumé?
   What are the disadvantages of using a professionally crafted résumé?
10. Is it also important for the job *holder* to have an up-to-date résumé? Explain.

CHAPTER 4

The Interview

The On-Target Interview

Here are pointers for putting your interview on target. The on-target interview hits the mark. It results in your being offered a job.

Consider These Do's

- Recognize that you are a salesperson with something unique to sell—yourself
- Learn the interviewer's name. Use it.
- Be prepared to state your mission when you arrive at the employment office.
- Have all needed items with you. Your social security card, for example—no, not just the number, the card. I can name three or four companies that will not talk job until they see the card.

  Bring along a résumé (a personal data sheet outlining your education and job achievements). While the résumé cannot and should not talk for you, it's comforting to know that you can check any necessary dates or other information. The preparation of a good résumé is so important that it is covered in a separate section.
- Have change for phone calls and parking. It's hard to maintain your poise while you ask for change.
- Come alone. Don't join forces with a friend. I have turned down many twosomes when I had only one job to offer. So has everybody else in the personnel field.

  Don't bring any relatives along. Your mother, father, wife, or husband may mean well, but *they* answer when you should. And yes, I've experienced all of the above.

Aunts, uncles, and—would you believe?—children, too.

- Do shake hands if a hand is offered. Grasp firmly. Don't break it but don't offer a limp, unfriendly, or shy hand.
- Stand until you're asked to sit.
- Do speak up and out. You can't expect the interviewer to wring questions and comments from you. If you've ever hosted a party, you'll agree—the most enjoyable guests are the contributors, not the ones you have to draw out or entertain. The same applies here.
- Know what the company does or makes. Here's where your prospect card helps.

  For example: If you apply for a job at Liebel-Flarsheim (maker of hospital equipment) don't tell them you always wear Florsheim shoes. I can vouch for that goof. An applicant said that to me when I did a special assignment there.

  I also had a Procter & Gamble job candidate urge me to hire her because she was so loyal to a particular brand of face soap (not ours). Remarks such as those are always good for a laugh, seldom for a job.
- Bask in the knowledge that personnel people love to hire applicants. It would warm your heart to know how with you the interviewer really is. Help her or him to help you by thinking of every possible thing you might do to aid the organization's progress or to solve its problems.
- Anticipate probable questions. That's easy to do if you'll study the section on interviewers' questions.

Review Questions

The On-Target Interview

1. What should you have with you at the time of the interview? Name at least three items.
2. Should you and your friend apply at the same time? Explain.

3. What are some of the questions interviewers ask? Give two questions that you expect to be asked.
4. Give your answers to two of the questions you expect to be asked.
5. Who has the responsibility for interview follow-up? The interviewer? The applicant?

The Off-Target Interview

Here are pointers on what to avoid if you do not want your interview to be off-target.

Consider These Don'ts

- Don't let distractions, such as a broken pair of glasses or a dangling toothpick, mar a good impression. Get the glasses fixed and get rid of the toothpick.
- Don't insist on making your interview at a time inconvenient for the interviewer.
- Don't ask for a job—or a chance. Come now, no salesperson talks that way, nor should you.
- Never say, "I'll take anything." Never. Instead (when you're very desperate) say something such as, "I've no quarrel with hard work. I can take what might seem to you a lowly job if there is a chance to move up and out as I prove myself."
- Don't apologize for lack of experience. Instead, talk about your trainability and about how quickly you learn.
- Don't try to do all the talking. When some of us get a bit nervous (most job applicants do), we try to cover our nervousness by talking too much.

  Your share of any conversation in which two persons are involved is roughly 50 percent. If you're part of a three-way interview, your share is about 33 percent. These percentages will vary according to the way the interviewer guides the interview.
- Do not try to prolong the interview. It is not up to you to do so.
- Do not smoke. Even if the interviewer smokes, do not

smoke. It's difficult to synchronize your cigarettes. All too often, you're just lighting up when the prospective employer would like to move on.

- If you're a drop-in candidate (and sometimes that's all right), don't do your dropping-in during lunch hour.
- Don't pop into an employment office five minutes before closing time and expect to land a job.
- Don't tell a prospective employer about all the turndowns you've had. Pessimism breeds pessimism.
- Don't wander from the subject at hand, which is *how the prospective employer can use your services*. When the interviewer strays just be charming in return.
- Don't insist on filling in a written application. Sometimes the employer is trying to save you hunting hours by not urging you to do so. Leave your résumé instead—make sure you have a good one.
- Don't rely too heavily on introductions or letters of recommendation. They only supply the entry. You should be very hesitant about accepting a job you didn't earn on your merits. "Easy hire, easy fire" is an old maxim in the personnel field.
- Don't act disgruntled if you are asked to take employment tests. It's a rare company that will take the additional time for tests unless it is serious about considering your qualifications.
- Avoid the What-do-you-have-for-me? approach. You really can't expect a prospective employer to rattle off a list of ways he or she can use your services.
- Don't let your handicaps handicap you. Talk only about your abilities, not your disabilities. I have hired blind candidates, deaf candidates, and crippled candidates, but *not once out of pity*.
- Don't kill yourself by "degrees." The but-I'm-a-college-graduate routine is very unappealing. I have a colleague who swears she actually responds by saying, "I won't hold that against you. Now what did you learn and what can you do for us with it?"

- Do not take more than one drink if you've been invited for lunch or dinner. Take that only if your host is having one. And there is *never* a need to take one if you don't want it. If you don't, simply order juice so that you won't seem to be telling your host what not to do.
- Don't hurt your prospective employer's ears. Ask someone you trust to point out your more obvious errors in grammar or word usage. And don't hate the person who is brave enough to comply with this request. You can't spot your own errors any more than you can proofread your own typing.

  While you're at it, also ask your critic and friend if you pepper your speech with *"you know."* A large number of younger applicants use this, and it grates on interviewers' ears until they want to scream, "No, I don't know."
- Do not hang around after the interview is over. How will you know when the interview is over? Usually the fact that the interviewer has ceased to ask questions and has thanked you for coming in signals the end of the interview. Occasionally, the glazed look in the eyes of the interviewer communicates this information.

Don't Become Discouraged. Instead, use your turndowns as learning opportunities. With each turndown, ask the person who interviewed you for a brief appraisal. Make a sincere request such as, "You're an experienced interviewer. Can you give me any tips to strengthen my next interview?" Be prepared to listen openly, actively, and without resentment to what comes next.

If you listen openly, you'll soon be on target with your interviews and on the payroll.

Review Questions

The Off-Target Interview

1. Why should you not tell an interviewer about how hard you've been looking?

2. What kinds of things could prove distracting in an interview? Name at least two.
3. Is it ever okay to just drop into an employment office? Explain.
4. What is the best time to arrange an interview?
5. How can you tell when the interview is over?
6. If the interviewer smokes, is it all right for the applicant to smoke? Explain.

Interview Questions

Here are some of the questions the prospective employer will ask you. (It is important to answer the question that is asked—not another one.)

- What do you know about us?
- What can you tell me about your current job?
- What do you think determines a person's progress in a good company?
- Are you looking for a permanent or a temporary job?
- Do you prefer to work with others, or do you prefer to work alone? Why?
- What percentage of your educational expenses did you earn? How?
- If you had a choice of any job, anywhere, what would you choose to do?
- What job in our company would you choose if you were given a choice?
- What job in our organization do you want to work toward?
- What jobs have you enjoyed the most? The least?
- Do you prefer a large or a small organization? Why?
- Have you ever declared bankruptcy? Are you bondable?
- What was your best subject in school? Your worst? Your favorite?
- Do you know anyone who has ever done the type of work under discussion?

- Why do you want to work for our organization? How did you happen to apply here?
- What are your goals? Long range? Short range?
- Will you tell me something about yourself?
- What are your strengths? Your weaknesses?
- Describe a crisis you had to deal with and tell me how you coped with it.
- What kinds of contributions could you make to our company?
- Why are you leaving your present employer?
- What is there about you that qualifies you for this position?
- In what ways did your education prepare you for this job?
- How would you evaluate your performance on your present job?
- Are you free to travel? To relocate? Do you have your own transportation?
- In what way is your previous experience applicable to the job for which you are applying?
- What do you think of your current management? (Or, how are they to work for over at X Company?)
- Why do you think this job will be better than the one you have?
- Whom do you envy? Whom do you admire?
- What kind of supervisor do you like best—one who spells things out or a delegator?
- If you had to describe yourself to another person, how would you do it?
- Have you any experience in this kind of work?
- How did you happen to choose this particular field of work?
- What about our product or service is of interest to you?
- Would you guess our margin of profit to be large? Small? Explain.
- What are the advantages of work in your chosen field? The disadvantages?

- Where do you see yourself in this company five years from now? Ten years?

Here are some of the questions you will want to ask the prospective employer.

- Is this a permanent job, or is it a training ground for something else?
- Can you tell me something about the last person who held this job?
- I recently read that Widget Company bought some land over in Vandalia. Are you free to tell me anything about plans for expansion?
- What is the future for this type of work here at Widget?
- Will you describe a typical day for me? That is, what would the daily duties for this job be?
- Does Widget have a policy of "promotion from within," or do you usually look to the outside for executive talent?
- What sort of person do you hope to hire for this position?
- What is the rate of turnover in this kind of work here at Widget? How does this turnover compare with other companies in this business?
- How does the present organization compare in size to the company of five years ago?
- How does this area of the company fit into the organizational whole? (You should know whether you're applying to the home office, district office, sales office, plant, or whatever.)
- Is this a new position, or would I be replacing someone? Where is that person?
- Am I under serious consideration?
- Will you tell me something about the supervisor? Does he or she like to give close supervision? Or is he or she a delegator?
- Please tell me the best and the worst about the job.
- Can you tell me something about the people in management? Would you say they are traditional? Contempo-

rary? A cohesive, homogeneous group? Family operated?
- Can you tell me something about company ownership?
- You probably have an established salary range for this position. Can you tell me what it is? (Ask this question only if you are asked about salary.)
- What is the purpose of this job?
- What does your organization hope to have the person you hire accomplish?
- What problems do you hope to have solved by the person you hire for this job?

Your questions can become more penetrating after you are offered a job. For example:
- Can you tell me a bit about your experience with the company?
- Will you tell me something about the supervisor to whom I'll report? (It's good personnel practice to see that you meet your future boss.)

If you apply to a nonprofit organization, *always* find out how that organization is funded, who funds it, and how long the funds are guaranteed.

There are certain questions that will *lessen* your chances of a job offer. Here are some of them:
- Do not ask, "Are you hiring?" That question puts the interviewer on the spot. In fact, I know several employers who always say no to that question whether or not they need employees. You see, the employer is afraid to say yes for fear he or she will then have to explain why a certain candidate wasn't hired. Some employers are actually afraid of being sued in such instances. *It has happened.* Instead of such a pointed question, express your interest in the company and in being interviewed.
- Do not ask, "Do you have an opening?" Better to say, "Are you accepting applications?"
- Do not ask, "What's wrong?" if you are turned down for a job. Instead ask, "How can I strengthen my next

interview?" This makes it easy for the interviewer to help you. This is another of those instances in which the interviewer is afraid to level with you for fear of your anger or a possible lawsuit.

- Do not ask, "Does this job lead to promotion?" You see, *jobs* don't lead to promotion. It's the *performance of a job* that leads to promotion.
- Do not ask, "What does this company make?" or "What does this organization do?" If you've done your homework, you'll know the answers to these questions. Your knowledge of the company should enable you to be more specific than that. Your presentation and questions in the interview should center around ways in which your contributions and abilities could benefit the organization.
- Do not ask, "Will you give me a job?" No one can *give* you a job, you must *earn* it. It's better to say you want to work rather than you want a job. Please note the distinction.

I have two reasons for suggesting these questions.

1. It encourages you to be responsible for part of the interview.
2. By finding out what the interviewer is seeking, you can explain that you're the person he or she is looking for.

The Follow-up

Most of the job seekers I know don't write or phone after the interview. That's why it's to your advantage to do so.

The follow-up letter or phone call serves the purpose of getting the potential employer to take another look.

It can:

- strengthen the good impression you made in the interview
- recover lost ground from a weak interview.

In either case, you gain.

Come with me for a moment to the interviewer's side of

the desk. Often that person is in a decision dither. Typical concerns are:

- your interest in the job
- how long you'll stay
- how you'll get along with others
- gaps in your employment history
- your attitude toward past employers
- the number of jobs you've held
- your social life and whether it affects your work life
- time lost from school or past jobs
- how well you like the community
- whether you are in easy commuting distance
- whether you are energetic
- whether you'll be content with the probable salary
- whether you make good use of your time
- whether you check facts carefully
- whether you make your own decisions
- whether you are a person who will help solve company problems or whether you are the sort of person who creates problems wherever you go

Look over what could be in the employer's mind. If you can straighten out any of those thoughts, do so in your follow-up. Or use this as an opportunity to say the bright thing that occurred to you on the way home from the interview.

If you have overcome any specific negatives, now is the time to say so: Did you do poorly on a typing test and have you since improved? Have you done something to bring your weight to acceptable standards? Say so. Weight is one of the many subjects the interviewer will not mention. It's all right for you to talk about it.

Check your follow-up to be sure it reflects your *enthusiasm for the job* and not *your anxiety about getting a job*.

I remember a follow-up letter that won a job for a young woman I had interviewed and rejected. It said:

Thanks again for the pleasant and informative interview.

While I know you were trying to discourage me because of my inability to drive, you didn't manage to suppress your own enthusiasm for the position of market research investigator. Consequently, I was more interested after our talk, not less so.

When I returned to Cleveland, I took driving lessons, obtained my driver's license, and drove all the way to Cincinnati.

I am at the home of my college roommate and will call you late Thursday to ask you to see me again.

Sincerely,
Annie Applicant

What did I do? The same thing you'd do. I referred Annie to the market research department along with a strong recommendation that they employ her. They did.

Sometimes just a simple thank-you note does wonders for your chances. The only time a follow-up becomes a turnoff is the time you put the interviewer on the spot or make your follow-up a "begging" opportunity.

The follow-up phone call can be just as simple and effective.

"Mr., Mrs., Miss, Ms. Spooner (have the right name and use the salutation preferred by the prospective employer). This is Andy Applicant. Thanks again for the pleasant interview Thursday."

Pause for answer.

"I'm calling to tell you I've given careful thought to the position of bookkeeper with Pyramid Company. I'm more interested than ever since I've talked with you."

Pause for the interviewer's comments.

"When do you plan to come to a decision?"

Wait for answer.

"All right. Since I may be difficult to reach, I'd like to call you then."

Doesn't it make sense for the follow-up to come from you? After all, you should be very difficult to reach, because you're *working full-time at finding a job.*

PART II

The Winner's Edge

CHAPTER 5

How Do You Rate?

Instead of my rating you as an applicant, why not try rating yourself? Answer the following questions. *Honestly.*

Applicant Checklist

1. Appearance

A. I am neat, clean, well-groomed, and appropriately dressed. I look my best when I apply for a job.

B. I look no better, no worse than the other candidates in the waiting room. My appearance is not a drawback.

C. I like to be comfortable. I don't bother with a tie. (If female, I wear pantsuits.)

D. I never really thought about it. Yes, I wear jeans. Note: If hats or sunglasses are worn to the interview, or if you use a toothpick, your answer is a D. It is all right for women to wear hats at the interview.

2. Speech

A. I am often complimented on my way with words. My voice (tone, pitch, diction) is pleasant.

B. I know my grammar is so-so, but I've made a practice of asking for help. I've asked my spouse, parent, colleague, child, or friend to tell me about any glaring errors.

C. Language doesn't interest me.

D. I'm weak when it comes to words or language.

3. Vocabulary

I avoid clichés

Yes ______________________ No ____________________

I do not say:

"salary commensurate with experience"
"I'll take anything"
"challenging position"
"chance for advancement"
"rewarding job experience"
"I like people."

Take one point off your total score if you use any of the above phrases. I included them because I want you to know interviewers are sick of hearing them.

4. Letters

A. I write a separate letter of application to each company. I have it checked for errors. It is neatly typed. I write to a person, not to a company.

B. I use the same letter for many companies. Each letter is individually typed.

C. I duplicate my letters of application.

D. My letters are handwritten. I don't ask anyone to look them over.

5. Résumé

A. I have a neatly prepared résumé. It contains a statement of objective. It tells not only *what* I have done but *how* I did it.

B. I use a professionally crafted résumé. Or, I followed a résumé outline I saw in a book.

C. I have a good résumé but it's not current.

D. I must admit my résumé is poorly done.

6. Follow-up

Yes, I follow up every interview with a phone call or note.

No, I don't bother.

7. Schedule

A. I make eighteen to twenty interviews per week.

B. I make eight to seventeen interviews per week.

C. I have no schedule.

D. I become so discouraged after a turndown that it takes me a week to get started again.

8. I use prospect cards.

Yes__________________ No__________________

9. I have all the necessary tools: social security card, birth certificate, grade transcripts or diploma, letters of recommendation, résumé, and any others needed. Allow one point for each tool.

10. My friends know I am looking.

Yes__________________ No__________________

11. I have taken a personal inventory of my skills, abilities, likes, dislikes, strengths, and weaknesses.

Yes__________________ No__________________

12. I always know the interviewer's name before the interview.

Yes__________________ No__________________

13. I can give a prospective employer at least fifteen reasons for employing me.

Yes__________________ No__________________

14. When I talk with X company, do I convince them I want a job with X company? Or, do I seem to want a job with any *company, be it X, Y, or Z?*

Yes__________________ No__________________

Scoring

Allow eight points for each *A* answer; six points for each *B* answer; *C* answers have no point value; *D* answers are minus five.

A answers for questions one and two are worth ten bonus points each.

Yes answers are worth eight points.

Rate Yourself

104 to 132—You'll have a good job offer within the week.
84 to 103—Reread this section. You'll increase your odds and have a good job offer within two weeks.
50 to 83—Ask someone you trust to help you improve your approach.
Under 50—Seek help from teachers, friends, job counselors, and the interviewers who turn you down.

Job Holder Checklist

Whether you're a beginning file clerk or a vice-president, someone is rating you. This test gives you the chance to do the rating yourself. Circle one answer for each item.

1. Value

How do I rate in terms of value to the organization?
A. I am the most valuable person in my department.
B. I'd rate among the top 25 percent.
C. I'd rate in the top 50 percent.
D. I'd rate in the lower 50 percent.

2. Appearance

A. I always present a well-groomed appearance.

B. I look no better, no worse than others in my department.

C. I am not so attractive as when I was hired (place a check mark here ____ if your weight is no longer in proportion to your height, if you've lost teeth that have not been replaced, etc.). Age is not a factor.

3. Attitude.

When I talk about my place of employment, I say
A. "my company."
B. "the company."
C. "they."

4. Do I Keep My Boss Informed?

A. Yes, I have developed a system for doing so.

B. I do so most of the time.

C. What I do is my responsibility.

5. Do I Make Suggestions?

A. I made an acceptable suggestion within the past month.

B. I often pass along suggestions to management.

C. I very seldom make suggestions.

D. I never make suggestions. If I did, they would be hostile.

6. Ability

A. My ability has improved markedly since I took this job.

B. I have taken outside training in order to improve my performance. Some of my reading material is job related.

C. I forget all about my work when I'm away from it.

7. Priorities

A. My priorities are in accord with those of my organization.

B. I think my priorities are in accord with those of my organization.

C. I don't know if my priorities are in accord with those of my organization.

D. We don't agree on what's important.

8. Where Am I?

A. I can usually be found at my place of business, i.e., my desk, my office, my place on the line.

B. Most of the time I'm where I'm supposed to be.

C. I hate to report on my every move.

D. I am often away. I make errands last as long as possible. My phone is uncovered more than ten percent of the time.

9. Attendance

A. My attendance is excellent. I miss no more than seven days a year.

B. I miss no more than twelve days a year.
C. Who knows how many days I miss each year?
D. I miss quite a few days.

10. Punctuality

A. I am punctual.
B. I am usually on time.
C. I am late when there are traffic or weather tie-ups.
D. I am often late.

11. Welcome Back?

If I left this organization and reapplied, would they take me back?

A. They would welcome me with open arms.
B. They would probably take me back.
C. I'm not sure if they'd take me back.
D. I doubt that they'd take me back.

12. Relationships With Others

If a congeniality award were given, I'd

A. win for my department.
B. place in the top 25 percent.
C. place in the top 50 percent.
D. place in the lower 50 percent.

13. Use of Language

A. I am often complimented for my clarity of speech. My speech never grates on the ears of others because I avoid obscenity, jargon, and do not make errors in grammar.

B. My speech and choice of words are better than average.

C. I never really thought about it.

D. Others often correct my speech.

Scoring

Allow eight points for each *A* answer; six points for each *B* answer; *C* answers have no point value; deduct five points for each *D* answer.

A answers for numbers 11 and 13 are worth ten bonus points each.

Rate Yourself

100 to 124—What a delight you must be.

84 to 99— You're a very satisfactory employee. There is room for growth.

50 to 83— Watch yourself in a tight labor market. Begin your program of improvement right away.

Under 50— There is hope for you. After all, you were interested enough to take this test. But drastic measures are needed or you will soon be fired.

How Do You Rate in the Eyes of the Interviewer?

Many, many interviewers still use rating sheets. Few will admit it. This rating sheet is a composite of those used by eight colleagues. No, I'll never tell you which companies are represented here. Obviously, no one company rates you on everything I show you here. You can relax—a little. No one I know keeps these rating sheets as a part of your permanent record.

Interviewer's Rating Sheet

Job candidate: ______________________________

Position desired: ______________________________

Appearance:

  Clothing:

  Good business taste

    Borderline ______

    Unsatisfactory ______

  Hands and face:

    Healthy looking ______

    Well cared for ______

    Poor complexion ______

    Heavy makeup ______

    Poorly cared for teeth ______

    Dirty ______

    Chewing gum ______

Attitude:

Enthusiastic	______	Abrasive	______
Attentive	______	Hostile	______
Unresponsive	______		
Negative	______		

Personality:

Magnetic	______	Tactless	______
Animated	______	Conceited	______
Pleasant	______	Disagreeable	______

Ability to Communicate:

Speech

Good grammar	______	Indistinct	______
Good diction	______	Poor grammar	______
Good vocabulary	______	Loud	______
Quiet	______	Uses jargon	______

Thoughts

Well organized ___
Average ___
Poor ___

Knowledge:

Knowledge of Company

Good comprehension ___
Poor comprehension ___
Uninformed ___

Knowledge of Job

Good comprehension ___
Poor comprehension ___
Uninformed ___

Sense of Responsibility:

Arrived promptly	_____
Was tardy	_____
Contributed to quality of interview	_____
Did not contribute to quality of interview	_____
Has history of acting responsibly	_____
Has history of acting irresponsibly	_____

Overall Rating:

Exceptional	_____
Above average	_____
Good	_____
Below average	_____
Poor	_____

Interviewer's Comments:

Recommendation:

Employ	_____
Hold file for future consideration	_____
Not recommended	_____

CHAPTER 6

Help for "Hear"-ache

"Hear"-ache can cost you a job.

Have you ever talked with someone who uses words or phrases that grate on your ears?

Yes?

Then you might wonder if words or phrases you use give someone else a "hear"-ache? Again the answer is yes. Sadly, we are unaware of our wince words.

All of us have developed selective hearing. What is selective hearing? It is our penchant to screen what we hear. Do you remember the little Connecticut girl who started the Lord's Prayer this way? "Our Father who art in New Haven, how did you know my name?"

That little girl did what most of us do all the time; she heard what she wanted to hear. Selective hearing also accounts for the new-word phenomenon. You've experienced this: You learn a new word one day and then hear it fifty times the next week. That word was around all the time, you simply had your ears closed to it. I make this point to illustrate that we screen our word errors this way.

Alas, our listeners do not use the same screen.

If we make only one speech error, chances are we make it one hundred times a week. That causes others to wince one hundred times.

Why am I sounding off about words in a book about jobs? Because I hope what I say here will serve as a reminder: How you sound is just as important as how you look when you apply for a job.

Oral Surgery: How to Remove Your Foot from Your Mouth

- Recognize that a single utterance can cost you a job. Now that I'm a free-lancer, I'm free to admit I decided against going further with the application of a secretary who said to me, "Somewhere*s* there must be a job for me." And I still wince over the candidate who said, "It *don't* matter where you put me, I *can't hardly* wait to get started." Did I tell either applicant the basis for the turndown? Of course not. It would have been poor public relations. Besides, I wasn't asked.
- Admit that you make mistakes. Vow to find out what they are and to eliminate them.
- Use the buddy system. Ask your spouse (who probably has your errors on tap), a co-worker, a teacher, your child, or a friend to help you spot your mistakes. Do the same for her or him *if asked.*
- Make flash cards of the words and phrases you want to eliminate. Carry the cards around until you rid yourself of the errors.
- Tune your ears to hear your wince words; at the same time learn to be more tolerant of those of others.
- Be sure you do not allow me or anyone else to ruin brisk, original speech.
- Learn to echo important messages. When you echo (say in your words) what you think you have heard, you save marriages, friendships, time, and gain promotions.
- Learn to use a dictionary as the editors intended. A dictionary *reports usage* so you will find many wince words there. You will see words such as *ain't* and *irregardless.* True, if you read the entire entry after each word, you will probably see that those words are considered substandard, irregular, or not considered acceptable by a panel of experts.

Unfortunately, many people take a quick look and report, "I saw it in the dictionary." So they give the word unmerited respect.

Know that the job of a lexicographer is to report usage—not to arbitrate usage.

- Rid your vocabulary of conversational tics and burrs. Each of us has a computer in his or her brain where we store words. Unless we take deliberate action to store crisp, fresh words there, the same tired words will come spilling out every time we talk.

Experts always tell us to increase our vocabularies, and that's good advice. But I'm about to give some *better* advice. Every time you add a new word to your vocabulary, make a real effort to throw out a tired, abused, or misused word or phrase. If you pepper your speech with "you know" or "that's for sure," or if you end sentences with "okay?" let those conversational tics and burrs be the first to go.

How to Rate the Effect of Your Speech on Others: An Instructive Test

Are you a pain in the ear? Most of us are—at least part of the time.

You've listened to other people for years. Take a few minutes now to listen to yourself. Ask yourself, "Do I give someone else a "hear"-ache? Do the words I use grate on someone else'e ears?"

Here's one way to tell. Answer the following questions. Honestly. Then check the rating scale.

1. I (can hardly, can't hardly) wait to hear from Widget Company.
2. It was a (heartrending, heartrendering) experience.
3. You (should of, should have) seen that bullfrog jump.
4. (As, Like) I told him yesterday, it won't work.
5. I am writing in (regard, regards) to your report.
6. Gerald Ford, (formerly, formally) a president of the United States, will introduce the speaker.

7. Has Eleanor been (apprised, appraised) of these changes in policy?
8. My son made a sky jump (once, onct).
9. Finneytown is (farther, further) from town than Clifton.
10. Don't let (perspiration, prespiration) spoil a fine garment.
11. We (were, was) planning to see a film.
12. Why not consider Arizona? I'm told the climate is (healthy, healthful).
13. Millie is a delightful (human, human being).
14. Carole was paid an unusual (compliment, complement).
15. The doctor explained the function of his (prostate, prostrate) gland.
16. I (suspect, suspicion) that she is the one.
17. She pronounces experiment "ek-spair- (to rhyme with air) uh-ment." He says, "ek-spear- (to rhyme with fear) uh-ment." Which is preferred?
18. I am (enthused, enthusiastic) about improving my speech.
19. Myself and Shirlie are going to town. OR Shirlie and I are going to town.
20. She sent a gift to Bruce and (I, me).
21. They have only (theirselves, themselves) to blame.
22. I hope this won't (recur, reoccur).
23. I am (averse, adverse) to the new tax law.
24. We shall refund your money (provided, providing) the merchandise has not been used.
25. Dear Mary, Fred and Joe, I hope (you, youse) can come to the party.
26. I am concerned about (errors in grammar, grammatical errors).
27. I seem to become (nauseous, nauseated) every time I have three milk shakes.
28. (Incidentally, Incidently), I am happy to respond to Jeff's request.

29. How has the ruling (affected, effected) your department?
30. From her comment, we (inferred, implied) that she was recovering.
31. Are the words oral and verbal interchangeable?
32. It (don't, doesn't) make any difference.
33. Where is it? OR Where is it at?
34. Who is the (principal, principle) of Western Hills High School?
35. This test (isn't, ain't) so difficult.
36. I (came, come) to the office yesterday.
37. She is light (complected, complexioned).
38. Tell me where to apply. Where is your (personnel, personal) office?
39. Do you know of a job opening (anywhere, anywheres) for me?
40. I am six feet two inches in (height, heighth).
41. I (am not, ain't) interested.
42. I am going to the fair (regardless, irregardless) of what you say.
43. This conclusion is not based on a single (criterion, criteria).
44. What do you mean to (imply, infer) by that statement?
45. I was (unaware, unawares) that he is married.
46. I want to study (preventive, preventative) medicine.
47. She has a (way, ways) to go.
48. It is thirty (mile, miles) from here.
49. He (et, ate) his dinner with us last night.
50. How do you pronounce the word chasm?
51. Radio is still my favorite (media, medium).
52. What is wrong with the following sentence? I shall continue on in the job after he is gone.
53. What is wrong with the following sentence? The advertising director suggested that we include a free gift.
54. That is my favorite (quote, quotation).

55. June 30 is the last day of our company's (fiscal, physical) year.

KEY

1. can hardly
2. heartrending (You render fat, not hearts.)
3. should have
4. As
5. regard
6. formerly
7. apprised
8. once
9. farther
10. perspiration (That first syllable is *per,* rhymes with her.)
11. were
12. healthful
13. human being
14. compliment
15. prostate
16. suspect
17. It is ek-spair- (to rhyme with air) uh-ment.
18. enthusiastic
19. Shirlie and I are going to town.
20. me
21. themselves
22. recur
23. averse
24. provided
25. you
26. errors in grammar (Grammatical means according to the rules of grammar, so you don't have grammatical errors.)
27. nauseated
28. Incidentally
29. affected
30. inferred
31. No. Verbal refers to either spoken or written words, while oral refers only to spoken words.

32. doesn't
33. Where is it?
34. principal (Remember that a principal is your pal, and you'll use the correct ending in this word.)
35. isn't
36. came
37. complexioned
38. personnel
39. anywhere
40. height
41. am not
42. regardless
43. criterion
44. imply
45. unaware
46. preventive
47. way
48. miles
49. ate
50. kaz'-um
51. medium
52. the word *on* is unnecessary
53. All gifts are free, so "*free* gift" is redundant.
54. quotation
55. fiscal (Do remember the word has two syllables, not three.)

Scoring

Start with 100 points.
Deduct two points for each incorrect answer.

Rate Yourself

90-100	You're a joy as a speaker.
80-90	You like words and enjoy using them correctly. You hurt other people's ears only about 10 percent of the time.
60-80	Chances are you're making more mistakes than you realize. Try to "proof heed" your speech as you would proofread something you've written.

40-60 You're jarring quite a few eardrums, but there is hope for you. You wouldn't be reading this book if you weren't interested in doing better. Ask a teacher, friend, or associate to help you.

Under 40 What you say and how you say it is hurting you more than you can imagine.

How to Choose the Words that Will Enhance Your Image

"All of a man's antecedents and possibilities are summed up in a single utterance, which gives at once the gauge of his education and his mental organization." Oliver Wendell Holmes.

Unless you don't want to appear smarter, richer, better-educated, more contemporary, and younger, you won't want to bother with this section at all.

Who are you?

The words that are stored in your word warehouse reveal a great deal about you. In fact, they reveal more than any regional accent you may have. Your word choices reveal whether you're young or old, whether your background was up-scale or down-scale, and whether you read a lot or very little.

The words we're going to talk about here are neither wrong nor right. But they do leave traces of where you've been and who you've been.

The idea for a collection of up-scale and down-scale words was triggered by Vance Packard's book *The Status Seekers.* Remarks by my psychology and sociology professors affected my status words.

Although this section began with what an authority said, it doesn't end there. All the revealing words (up-scale words, down-scale words, dated words, new words, old words, young words, rich words, poor words) have been people-tested—from Maine to California, from Miami to Michigan.

My informal sample includes college professors, secretaries, teachers, scientists, lawyers, doctors, bankers, homemakers, a twelve-year-old neighbor, and my ninety-two-year-old aunt.

My formal sample includes everyone who has ever taken a word workshop I give called Help for "Hear"-ache.

I owe you one other admission. This aspect of my word watching was not intended to be serious (that is, in the beginning). It was intended to be used as fill-in lecture material. At first I used it sparingly and somewhat apologetically, for it is not the usual fare of a language course. But, the participants tell me, it should be an important part of every language course.

Am I saying that the outcome of an interview or the chance for a promotion could hinge upon your choice of words?

Yes, I am saying just that. When you come right down to it, your romance could too. Indeed, all your relationships are affected by your choice of words.

The words that follow do not represent a complete list. I merely want to ignite your thinking. I want you to ask: "What am I telling about myself each time I open my mouth?"

MINUS WORDS These words detract from your image.	PLUS WORDS These words enhance your image.
a hold of	reach
air corps	air force
bathing suit	swimsuit
bawl out	scold, reprimand
better half	wife, husband

MINUS WORDS	PLUS WORDS
blackboard	chalkboard (Black is no longer the prevailing color of chalkboards.)
bride and groom	bride and bridegroom
British citizen	British subject
butcher	meat cutter
cake of soap	bar of soap
car wreck	car accident
Chief Justice of the Supreme Court	Chief Justice of the United States*
claim	say
clap	applaud
cleaning woman	domestic
colored, Negro	Black or Afro-American
cuss	curse
deaf and dumb	deaf, hearing-impaired (Most persons who have hearing impairments do speak.)
dig an oil well	drill an oil well
dishrag	dishcloth
drapes	draperies

MINUS WORDS	PLUS WORDS
eats	food
electric (as "The electric is off.")	electricity or electric power
ex-husband	former husband
fireman	firefighter
gal	woman
girl friend, boy friend	friend
graduated	was graduated from
grip	bag, baggage, suitcase
hair—One sometimes refers to hair and incorrectly says, "shampoo them."	hair—Shampoo *it,* not *them,* is correct.
half-a-dollar	fifty cents
heavyset	overweight
home (as an edifice)	house
honeymoon	wedding trip
hub caps	wheel covers
icebox	refrigerator
idiot	developmentally disadvantaged
lame	crippled, handicapped, disabled

MINUS WORDS	PLUS WORDS
machine (for automobile)	automobile, car
maiden name	birth name
manpower	human energy, human power
material, goods	fabric
the missus, the mister	my wife, or Mrs. Martin, or Phyllis; my husband, or Mr. Martin, or Bruce
movies	films
of a night	at night
out loud	aloud
passed away	died
piano player	pianist
picture (when you mean painting)	painting
postman	mail carrier
Reverend or Rev. Foster	the Rev. Mr. (or Dr.) Foster
Sahara Desert	Sahara (Sahara means desert so you don't need to repeat the word.)
sassy	saucy
shot	injection

MINUS WORDS	PLUS WORDS
Sierra Mountains	Sierras (Mountains is inherent in Sierras, of Spanish derivation, so you don't need to say mountains twice.)
Smithsonian Institute	Smithsonian Institution
soprano singer	soprano (It is all right to refer to a soprano saxophone.)
square	block
stewardess	flight attendant
tease (as hair)	back comb
They got married.	They were married.
tux	black tie
undertaker	funeral director
unwed mother	single mother
vet	veterinarian, or doctor of veterinary medicine
wash rag	washcloth
Wimpleton	Wimbledon, pronounced wim-*b*ull-*d*on (if you are referring to the site of the famous tennis matches).
women's lib	women's liberation

*Note: The correct mode of address is so important and so intricate that you'll probably want to consult an etiquette book for a complete list.

Many manufacturers have lost their trademarks as a result of indiscriminate use of brand names. Limit your use of the following names to those times when you refer to the product or manufacturer in question.

Band-Aid	adhesive bandage
Clorox	bleach
Coca-Cola	cola
Coke (Coke is a registered name for Coca-Cola.)	cola
Davenport (This word is now considered old-fashioned.)	sofa, divan
Fiberglas	fiber glass
Formica*	laminated plastic
Frigidaire	refrigerator
IBM	computer
Jell-O	gelatin
Kleenex	facial tissue
Magic Marker	felt-tipped pen
Scotch tape	cellophane† tape or transparent tape

Teleprompter	prompting device
Thermos	vacuum bottle
Vaseline	petroleum jelly
Xerox	copier

*The manufacturers of Formica almost lost exclusive rights to their famous trademark because people grew careless and referred to all laminated plastic as Formica. It took congressional action to save the word. See why manufacturers wince when you misuse their trademarks?
†The word cellophane was originally Cellophane, a trademark. The manufacturer lost exclusive rights to the word because people used it as a generic term.

The Forty-five **Worst** *Words and Phrases to Use in the Presence of Managers and Personnel Directors*

The following words and phrases constitute a very special list. These words received the largest number of votes in an unpopularity test. Voters were managers and personnel directors.

The words you see here were culled from a list of 560 abused and misused words. Each participant was asked to choose five words or phrases for elimination. There were approximately six hundred participants. Tests were conducted over a two-year period. Not all participants obeyed instructions; instead of selecting five words for elimination, some chose to cast five votes against one or two words. The starred words received the largest number of nay votes.

Many place names received write-in votes. Illinois—when pronounced ill-ih-noi*s*, sounding the s at the end—hurt many ears. So did Cincinnati when pronounced sin-sin-at-*uh*. It is, of course, pronounced sin-sin-at-ee. So many places were mentioned that I must add this bit of advice: If you want to live or work there, check with the chamber of commerce on how to say the name.

accidently	Outdated spelling of *accidentally.* Use *accidentally* (pronounce all five syllables).
*ain't	This is not standard English.
alright	Use *all right.*
and	Do not use instead of *to*; for example, come to see me, not come and see me.
anxious	Means to be worried, apprehensive. Do not confuse with *eager* (wanting very much).
anywheres	Drop that *s.*
at	Do not use at the end of a sentence; for example use *where* but not *where at.*
boughten	Use *purchased.*
*can't hardly	No, no. It is *can hardly. Can't hardly* is a double negative.
Clean up to here	Do not use to describe degree.

Clear up to here

Do not use to describe degree.

*Come

Do not use come when you mean came. For example, I came yesterday, not I come yesterday.

Dezember

The word is December. There is no *z* sound in the word or in the spelling.

enthused

Colloquial. Use *enthusiastic.*

*excape

The word you want is escape. It does not contain an *x*. Sound the *s*.

*e*k* cetera for *et* cetera

That first word is *et* (it rhymes with bet).

One executive penned this remark: "When I hear *ek* cetera, I know the person is not college trained."

experiment

Ex-*spare*-uh-ment is correct; ex-*spear*-uh-ment is incorrect.

Eyetalian

It is *It*alian. The first syllable rhymes with kit.

granted

Grant-ed. Do not say or confuse with *granite.*

healthy

Means having good health.

healthful	Means the conditions that promote good health.
heighth	There is no such word. The word is *height* (rhymes with kite).
hisself	The correct word is *himself.*
*I	Do not use when you mean *me* as in, "She gave the money to Barbara and me."
incidently	The word is *incidentally,* and it has five syllables.
irregardless	The word is *regardless.* Forget the *ir.*
*it don't	A contraction for *it do not.* Use *it does not* or *it doesn't.*
*manufacture	Man-*you*-fact-yoor is correct; man-*uh*-fac-ture is incorrect.
*me	Do not use as subject; for example, Kent and I are going, not Kent and me are going.
mischievous	Look at the last syllable and you'll say it correctly. It has only three syllables, and the last one is *vous,* it is not *ve-ous.* Say mis-chi-*vas.*

*myself	Do not use in place of *I;* for example, *Barbara and I are in accord,* not *Barbara and myself are in accord.*
nauseous	Means causing nausea. It was a nauseous situation; I am nauseated.
nuclear	Say noo-*klee-ur.* It is not noo-*ku-ler.* (Yes, I know the late President Eisenhower mispronounced the word, but no one outranked him so no one could (or would) correct him.)
onct	Please say once (no *t* in this word).
perspiration	*Per*-spir-a-tion is correct; *pres*-pir-a-tion is incorrect.
picture	Pik-*chur* or pik-*tyoor* are correct; pit-chur is incorrect.
preventative	*Preventive* is preferred.
realtor	This word has two syllables, not three. It is real-*tor.* Not re-*la-tor.*
reoccur	The correct word is *recur.*
somewheres	There is no final *s.* The word is *somewhere.*

theirselves	The word is *themselves*.
undoubtably	The word is undoubt*ed*ly.
worsh	The word is *wash* (no *r* in the spelling or in the pronunciation).
wrench	A tool. Never use it when you mean rinse.
*youse	No, no, no. The plural of you is you.

If you feel that your misuse of words is holding you back, or if you want more examples of plus and minus words, you can find help in a book that I wrote several years ago. It's called *Word Watcher's Handbook: A Deletionary of the Most Abused and Misused Words,* and it's available for $3.95 plus $1.00 postage and handling from the publisher, David McKay Company, Inc., 2 Park Avenue, New York, New York 10016.

Want a few more hints on plus and minus words? Here's a column from Ann Landers that contains several new examples:

Phyllis Martin has a few words for Ann Landers

DEAR ANN LANDERS: Why all the fuss because a TV news commentator says, "Febyooary," when all around us we hear "cold slaw," "sherbert," "realator," and "irregardless"—to mention just a few nerve grinders? The abuse of the English language has become so commonplace that our ears will soon be accustomed to non-words and atrocious usage. Please do your bit by printing this, Ann. I'm signing myself—In Need Of Earmuffs.

DEAR EAR: Funny you should write today. I just read a book by Phyllis Martin, a Cincinnati job counselor and business consultant and a columnist for the Cincinnati Post. It's "Word Watcher's Handbook" (McKay, publisher, a paperback, $3.95). While the author didn't say anything about "cold slaw," "sherbert," or "realator," "irregardless" was listed right up with words that are obsolete.

Phyllis also tells us it is better to say "over" than "overly." She asks that we avoid "over with." Just plain "over" will do.

"Personal friend" is one word too many. "Friend" is enough. The same goes for "personal opinion." If it's your opinion, it's personal.

Anyone who says "needless to say" is saying too much. If it was needless, you wouldn't be saying it.

"Muchly" was O.K. a few hundred years ago but it's a bit much now.

Don't say "enthused" when you mean "enthusiastic."

The word is "famous," not "famed."

"Fantastic" is probably one of the most overworked words of our time. Get out of the rut and look up synonyms. You will be surprised to discover what the word fantastic really means.

"Gentlemen"—not "gent," please.

"Heartrendering" is not a word. It's "heartrending." Fat is rendered, not hearts.

"At this point in time" and "frame of reference" are children of Watergate and everybody is sick to death of them.

"Gross" is overused, especially by the young. Try "vulgar" or "coarse."

The phrase "I don't think" is another dud. How can you express an opinion if you don't think? Say instead, "I think not."

"Hisself" is not a word. "Himself" is what you are after.

"Learning experience" doesn't mean anything. Either you learn from experience or you don't.

Not all "h's" should be dropped, as in "honorable." Don't say "umble," say "humble."

"Unbeknownst" is a pompous substitute for the simple word "unknown." Don't be stuffy.

Phrases that grate from overuse are, "You can say that again"—"See what I mean"—"Due to the fact"—"How about that?" (You can also add to the list, "Have a nice day," and "Is it hot enough for you?")

Some of the most often mispronounced words are "knew"—it's not "noo," it's "nyoo." "Jewelry" is not "jool-ry." It's "jew-el-ree"—THREE syllables. "Prohibition" is "PRO-I-BI-SHUN." THE "h" is silent.

How many of you readers learned something today? I did. The book is fantastic—er—uh—I mean I'm enthused—pardon me—enthusiastic about it.

Reprinted by permission of Ann Landers.

CHAPTER 7

Helpful Hints

Thirty Tips to Increase Your Chances of Getting a Job

- There is no job classification called *anything*. Tell the employer what you can do *for* the organization.
- The responsibility for follow-up is with you, the job seeker, not the prospective employer. You're the one who's selling services. Remember?
- The superior job candidate knows how to fill an organizational gap before it becomes an opening. This is done by explaining how you would solve a company problem or meet a company need if they put you on the payroll.
- You are the most important product you will ever sell. Package yourself attractively.
- A single utterance can cost you a job. Eliminate abused and misused words from your speech.
- If you can make a copy of the company's application beforehand, do so. Filling in the copy will help you to do a better job on the real one. You'll also have a permanent record of what you said on the form.
- You double your chances of having a phone call about a job offer if you list two numbers—yours and a number where a message can be left.
- The job seeker has no corner on nervousness. Sometimes the interviewer is nervous, too.
- The nonverbal message is the one that is believed.

- You'll never be a winner in a contest you haven't entered.
- When there's a hairline's difference between candidates, the neater hairline wins.
- If you've no experience, don't apologize. Just say you've nothing to unlearn.
- Male job seekers: Increase your chances for a job by applying for jobs considered traditionally female.
- Female job seekers: Increase your chances for a job by applying for jobs considered traditionally male.
- If you hope for nothing from luck, chances are you will be so prepared, forewarned, forearmed, and open to opportunity that all shallow observers will call you lucky.
- Don't go job hunting in pairs. You cut your chances in half.
- There's no magic in Monday. It is usually not the best day to seek a job because it's the busiest day in the interviewer's week. Select another time to meet (unless the interviewer suggests Monday).
- Describe the job you think you are accepting to the interviewer. This saves confusion for both of you.
- Interviewers are tired of hearing, "I like people." Dogs like people, too, but that doesn't qualify them for a public relations assignment.
- Personnel people want to hire you. Make it easy by suggesting the benefits to them if they do hire you.
- Looking for a job is a job. Give it all the time and energy you have.
- Don't ask for a job. Ask for work.
- Don't be afraid to reapply to the same company.
- Don't come away from an interview empty-handed. Leave with a job offer, a clear-cut idea about follow-up, an appraisal if you've been turned down (the appraisal should outline ways to strengthen your next interview), or a referral to another company.

- Many companies will not process an application form unless your signature is on it.
- Carry your own pen with you when you apply for a job; those that you find in employment offices are of one quality—awful.
- Think about where you don't want to work as well as about where you do want to work.
- Every job seeker should have a master application form filled out. This will save possible embarrassment when you're faced with a real one. Be sure you have entered correct names of former employers, as well as the correct addresses and phone numbers of your schools. Some of you will want to have a record of the names and addresses of your spouse's or parents' employers too.
- Be creative about the way you apply for a creative job.
- Expenses incurred while looking for a job are tax deductible if the area of search is in the same field as your present or previous employment. If you're seeking a job for the first time, your expenses are not deductible even if employment is secured.

Thirty-five Tips to Help You Get Ahead Once You've Got the Job

- Capability, not chronological age, is the true measure of a worker's worth.
- Never allow the limits of what has been in the past determine what will be in the future.
- It's not enough to tell a worker what to do; explain why the job is being done.
- It seldom pays off to discuss pay with another worker.
- Some sacrifices are necessary in every job.
- If your employer doesn't offer a retirement plan, talk to a banker about starting your own. Specifically, ask about IRAs (individual retirement accounts) and Keogh plans.
- Take special care of equipment that everyone uses, and

always let the proper person know when supplies run low.

- Thank everyone who helps you. Thank them loudly and publicly.
- It's better to ask for more responsibility and more work than it is to ask for more money.
- Keep fit. You service your car, don't you? Do as much for yourself.
- Success is a positive attitude. More people are fired for a poor attitude than all other reasons combined.
- Always thank your boss for a raise. Your next one will come much faster if you do.
- The poorest reason to ask for a raise is because you need one. Ask for a raise only after you have earned it.
- Just because you have found a job is no reason to quit looking for work.
- Certain jobs don't lead to promotion. It is the way you perform a job that leads to promotion.
- You haven't found the right job until you get lost in your work.
- Concentrate on the strengths of those under you.
- Select people under you with the utmost care. If they're smarter, fine. As they push up the ladder of success, they push you, too, because there you are, a rung above.
- Echo all important messages. Say in your words what you think you heard.
- Be where you can be reached. You may never know how often your supervisor looked for you. How can you, if you just disappear?
- Tranquilizing periods are better than tranquilizing pills. For example, if you arrive five minutes early in the morning, you can carry that extra five minutes with you all day. The opposite is also true. If you're late for the first appointment of the day, you'll be late for all the others, too.
- Here's one way to spot a good employee: Others do

more work—not less—when he or she is around.

- Some workers carve a career; others chisel.
- If you must leave your job, don't have temper tantrums on the way out. You may want to reenter that same door.
- Don't let your supervisor be surprised. Keep him or her informed.
- Set challenging goals, and work toward meeting your goals.
- Let your supervisor know that you have challenging goals and are working toward meeting them.
- Set priorities, and always do the most important jobs first.
- It isn't enough to do a job well. The job must be worth doing in the first place.
- It's a rare worker who has listened himself out of a promotion.
- Be sure you're underpaid. In other words, do more than you are paid to do.
- Cut your worrying down to one day a week. Then you can concentrate on important worries and forget the others.
- Learn about your supervisor's job priorities. Tackle those jobs first.
- Learn to anticipate. Only those who learn to anticipate the future are prepared to handle it.
- Read. Inform yourself about world events, local events, developments in your field of work and in your company.

CHAPTER 8

How to Turn Rejection Into Positive Direction

Why do we dread rejection when it's supposed to be so good for us? I don't know. And the *why* is not the subject, not for this chapter anyway. We'll leave the *whys* to the wise psychologists.

The subject for this chapter is the leap from rejection to joy. And this leap starts where some of the most gigantic leaps start—from a low-down position, near the ground, often a kneeling position, *never a crawling one.*

Can you train for rejection? Yes. Actually, training is the first step.

As with all leaps and all successes, you must recognize they are possible. Take the case of the under-four-minute mile. For countless years no one managed it because no one thought a human being could run a mile in less than four minutes. But Roger Bannister must not have known the part about its being impossible because he did it. On May 6, 1954, at Oxford, England, Roger Bannister ran a mile in 3 minutes and 59.4 seconds. The world was astounded, but not for long. Because once it was known to be possible, others did it, too. On June 21 that same year, John Landy ran the mile in 3 minutes and 58 seconds. But before we leave the Roger Bannister incident, I want to comment on another aspect of this remarkable man's career. Roger Bannister lost only one race (and it was not to the man who broke his record). No, Roger Bannister beat John Landy in a subsequent race. The race he lost? His first.

So, we prepare for rejection by realizing that it happens to *every* human being at some time. Absolutely no one is immune. Every one of the fifty-thousand-plus job seekers I've interviewed has experienced it. I have too. It's a cozy feeling to know I have a lot of company in the rejection department. So have you. Did you know:

- that the Wright brothers' history-making flight was not even mentioned in the Dayton papers? (It's true that some out-of-town papers carried the story, but Dayton was unimpressed with Daytonians Orville and Wilbur at the time.)
- that Benjamin Disraeli (twice prime minister of Great Britain) was so mocked on his first speech in the House of Commons that he was forced to sit down? As he did so, he said, "I sit down now, but the time will come when you will hear me."
- that Miss U.S.A. of 1978, Judi Andersen, once entered a beauty pageant in Atlanta and didn't even place?

Expecting rejection makes it easier to take. Truly, it does. So, let me tell you what to expect. If you use a yardstick—it's twenty solid interviews for one *good* job offer—you won't become so downhearted with the first two or three turndowns. Many job seekers are ready to throw in the towel at this point. Don't. You're just getting started.

Contrary to popular belief, rejection *does not* sap your energy. Just the opposite. You're stimulated by it, and the energy generated by rejection is usually called resentment. If you don't believe me, just read the headlines for a day or two, and you'll agree that the rejected ones are practically galvanized to action. Here are two sample headlines:

- Rejected Job Seeker Kills Mayor
- Husband Shoots Estranged Wife When Reconciliation Attempt Fails

So, when you feel that flow of adrenaline after a turndown, get moving, in a positive direction. Otherwise you'll self destruct.

Some positive moves would be these:

- Find out why you were rejected. This will take some finesse. You don't just shout, "O.K., so what's the matter with me?" That's too negative, and it won't work anyway because you're putting the other person on the spot. Instead, try this: say, "Can you tell me how I can strengthen my next interview?" In most instances, you will have talked with a seasoned interviewer—a person who has an objective view of your strengths and weaknesses. Don't waste all the time you spent being appraised. Use it to your advantage. And when that interviewer is gutsy enough to level with you, do something constructive with the information. Improve your use of words. Lose those ten pounds. Quit chomping on your chewing gum. Dress in a more businesslike manner. Whatever.
- Next, ask the person who rejects you for referrals. You see, that interviewer feels guilty and wants to help. *I know*. It's an actual release to be able to do something for a person you've turned down. Besides, job interviewers know where the jobs are.

Reminders

- Rejection is contagious. You're going to have to admit this if you're to keep it from spreading from one area of your life to another. The fact that your husband walked out and left you does not make you an undesirable employee. The opposite is often true: A single person can offer more flexibility to an employer. Stress this flexibility (in time and with regard to possible relocation) to the prospective employer. Even your need for a job can become an asset (i.e., if your need for a job makes you more responsive to ways you can help the employer).
- Don't talk about your turndowns. If you tell an interviewer that you're being turned down all over town, it lessens your chances. Sometimes I've thought a candi-

date was top-notch until such a remark set me to wondering, "Hmmm, what are *they* discovering about this person that I'm not perceptive enough to see?" Not wanting to put a mistake on the payroll, I'd say no too.

- Sometimes the person or the company that turns you down isn't good enough to appreciate you. Mull that one over for a while. It's often true. Sometimes a job seeker is so high-powered that the interviewer knows there is no way to slot such a person. So if a small company turns you down, look to the large one, and if the large company turns you down, think of the glories of working for a smaller organization. Or consider a different kind of organization, perhaps one that is more creative.
- *Rejection is a form of release.* I hope your rejection releases you to do or be something far better than you've ever before dreamed.

PART III

The Finishing Touches

CHAPTER 9

How the Family and Friends of the Job Seeker Can Help

You can *do* so much and *undo* so much in your job seeker's campaign.

Surprised?

You shouldn't be. For when any person becomes a job seeker, that person becomes exceptionally vulnerable to everybody—especially you.

How can you help?

You can be understanding when the job seeker growls at someone in the household for hanging on the phone longer than five minutes. Waiting for *the* phone call is a trying experience. Even a five-minute wait while someone chats can seem interminable to the one waiting.

You can lift sagging spirits by providing a small surprise such as:

- a good map of the city
- a bus schedule
- a new pen or two
- new pencils with good erasers
- an alarm clock
- adequate change for parking, bus, or phone calls

You can give positive support by:

- providing names of prospective employers
- providing help with research about prospective employers via study of the complete newspaper, library research, study of annual reports and business

publications, and the telephone (obtain interviewers' names from the company operator)

You can help with the actual work of finding work by:

- typing résumés
- typing letters of application
- taking accurate phone messages—intelligently. This is a chance to be doubly sure of an employer's name and its pronunciation
- providing an organized work area

Small Comforts

You can give serious thought to the seemingly small creature comforts of the job seeker. You can perform special acts of kindness. For example:

- Rub a tired back.
- Provide a foot bath for burning feet.
- Clean shoes and see to their repair.
- See to special washing or dry cleaning.
- Have the car cleaned and the tank filled.
- Offer to be a chauffeur for a day or two. Looking is such a lonely business.
- Plan a culinary delight.
- Meet your job seeker for a *quick* lunch and get lost afterward. Helping to waste time is no favor. Of course, you'll rejoice if your applicant has to break the date for one with a prospective employer.
- Listen actively to a recital of "the rounds."
- Offer constructive comments—*if* asked.

And bite your tongue if you must but refrain from making killer comments such as the following. All of these comments have actually been reported to me by job seekers.

- Haven't you found anything yet?
- When you come home with a paycheck, then you can have some say around here.
- They tell me jobs are plentiful.
- Now don't be nervous.

- I've never liked you in that color.
- I wish you had time to get a haircut before your appointment.
- So-and-so found a job. I don't see why you can't.
- You might do something about the fit of that suit. (This was said as the applicant walked out the door on his way to a scheduled interview.)

Finally, you can show your abiding faith. By this time, the job seeker is hungry for it. As you know, it is the least lovable child who needs the most loving. So it is in the work world—the person who is without a job is the one who most needs your respect, love, and faith as never before.

For the Person in Personnel

Working with job applicants has convinced me that the personnel representative has more impact on the life of the applicant than almost anyone save family members and teachers. This tremendous impact is not a part of every employment encounter, but it occurs often enough to be truly awesome. What, then, can the personnel representative do to help the applicant?

Little helps. You can provide a warm and welcoming waiting room. My dream waiting room would have (in addition to the usual chairs, desks, and tables) a large map of the city and a rack containing:

- company literature
- literature about other local companies
- information on and from the public libraries
- information on and from the chamber of commerce (I'd buy any lists of corporations, corporate officers, and chamber members they'd sell to me.)
- literature on how to apply for a job
- address of the nearest state employment bureau
- a directory of major buildings. (Job hunters often do not know where major buildings are located.)
- a telephone directory for applicant use

- copies of the daily newspapers—open to the business or want-ad sections. Near this I would place pencils and little slips of paper such as the library uses.
- small candy mints

Big helps

Your courtesy. The applicant's time is important, too. Needless procrastination is rude. The courtesy of privacy and confidentiality also is appreciated.

Your honesty. It is kinder to say, "We won't call you unless something unexpected develops" than it is to say, "We'll call," and then not do so.

As a new interviewer, I used to say, "We'll call you *if* something develops." Finally, it dawned on me that nothing after the "we'll call" ever registered. So if the chance for employment is slim, say so—clearly.

Most applicants are understanding when you level with them.

Your knowledge. If you know of an opening somewhere else for which the applicant is better suited, say so. Or, if you have no opening, try to suggest possibilities in another company. If you can spare her or him a fruitless trip and another turndown, by all means do that, too.

The decision to give the true basis for disqualification is governed by whether the applicant will use the information constructively. Be guided by the applicant.

Your fairness. When the answer must be no, say it as quickly and kindly as you can.

If you can't be objective with a particular candidate, have someone else do the interviewing.

Your hope. While it would be useless to hold out hope for a job you can't offer, at least offer hope of another sort. Direct the attention and the feet of your candidate to other leads.

If you know of no other jobs, you might simply suggest, "Do you want to look over our newspaper and literature for other possibilities while you're here?"

Anything to direct the applicant's thinking *from* your company and *toward* something constructive is helpful.

Every candidate should be convinced that he or she has had an intelligent hearing.

CHAPTER 10

Special Problems

Too Young?

"We were really thinking of someone older."

Every young job seeker hears that tiresome phrase or a variation of it. "Ugh," you say, and I don't blame you. It *is* sickening to be met with that turnoff, or the one that goes, "We need an experienced person."

What can you do?

Plenty.

You can talk about the advantages of hiring someone your age—*with your strengths.* Then talk about *experiences you do have.* And you can dazzle them with visions of *services you can render.*

Your strengths:

- enthusiasm
- flexibility
- willingness to accept a smaller salary than the experienced worker
- trainability. Say, "I have nothing to unlearn," as one smart candidate did to me. Then add (as she did), "Your training will pay dividends because I intend to be around a while."

Tell about your experiences:

- baby-sitting jobs
- life guarding you've done
- work in the school office
- yard work
- contests you've entered (such as science awards contests and county fair projects)

Services:

Is your typing something special? I hired Delores C. (her real name) although I was not looking for a typist. Why? Because she brought samples of what she had done on a VariTyper in her high school business machines class. They were works of art.

I also hired a young man for yard maintenance because that is his specialty and because he sold me with a brochure about himself. On it he listed under "Work":

"Pruning: trees, shrubs, vines.

Tree-cutting: firewood, log steps, log furniture, log sections, patios and posts.

Grass-cutting: trimming, mulching, fertilizing, planting, pesticide, herbicide."

And that's not all by a long shot. He had ten categories under "Landscaping" and seven under "Buildings."

He did what I recommend to any job seeker of any age: *When you can't find a job, make one.*

Too Old?

If you think you're too old, you are.
If you think you are not, you aren't.

The best news to come out of the Fair Employment Practices Act is this: "It is unlawful to require a birth certificate or baptismal record before hiring."

Wait a minute. Before you decide to lop ten years off your age, you should also know this: "It is lawful to require proof of age by birth certificate after hiring."

Suppose you are asked your age. What then? You can always do as I do—say to the nervy one: "I'll be glad to tell you my age. But first, will you tell me why you need that information?"

If you are asked by a prospective employer, you can add (with your eyebrows up to your hairline in surprise), "In view of the Fair Employment Practices Act, I'm surprised your company would want you to ask." Blame it on the company; never blame the interviewer.

If you can manage a smile while your eyebrows are still arched in surprise, all the better. That act will, I guarantee you, finish the age question.

A Good Age. Now then, let's concentrate on why your age is such a good age. Muster some enthusiasm about it. Every age brings its compensations. If you are enthusiastic about where you are in life, you will transmit that enthusiasm to your prospective employer—and to just about everyone else you meet.

You like your age because:

- You have developed a sense of direction. You have a goal. This alone will cause you to look forward—not backward.
- You have developed judgment.
- You have developed good work habits.
- You are dependable.
- You need less training.
- You are unencumbered.
- You are flexible (tell how—by working irregular hours, for example).
- You are realistic.

Where to Look. Often the younger companies welcome the older worker. They need the older worker's seasoned judgment and advice.

Smaller companies are more likely to hire older workers than are larger companies. (Often large companies are busy retraining the older workers they already have for reassignment.)

The government shows no prejudice.

Check with service organizations of all kinds—social, religious, health, and private. Free-lance, consult, or teach special courses. Name it and I'll tell you about some older person who is doing it successfully.

What You Can Do. Almost everyone I've ever counseled

(especially women) has overlooked real contributions he or she has made.

Often I hear, "Oh, I didn't think you'd be interested in that" or "but that wasn't a real job." Dredge it up, look at it, and then decide if it's worthwhile.

Examine all these areas for clues: schooling, paid jobs, volunteer jobs, committee assignments, amateur theatricals, hobbies, travel.

Have you ever organized a garage sale, supervised a church supper, been a scout leader, headed a fund-raising drive, worked in an election campaign?

Come on now, really think.

Check your résumé. Does it make you sound vital, vibrant, aware? Or does it make you seem an "old-timer"? Recent schooling and active hobbies (such as swimming, hiking, or tennis) can reflect youthful zest.

Listen to yourself. Are your words outdated? Do you say "blackboard"? The newer word is "chalkboard." Do you say "stewardess"? Now it's "flight attendant." It's also "mail carrier." Not "mailman."

Why is this important? Am I nit-picking? Not really. I just want you to reflect the idea that you accept the challenge of change rather than cling to old ways. Don't be the kind of person who says, "In my day we did such-and-such."

It grieves me when people sixty-five, fifty-five, forty-five, or thirty-five consider themselves old.

Let me ask you something: Do you think Dinah Shore's producers consider her old?

No, she's just Dinah, a beautiful, vibrant woman. She's more attractive and younger now than when she graduated from Vanderbilt University in 1938.

We forget that "length of days" was considered a peculiar and cherished blessing in biblical times.

Too Old for What? We forget that:

- General Douglas MacArthur was in his seventies when

he served as Supreme Commander of the Occupation in Japan.

- Thomas Edison built chemical plants after he was sixty-seven.
- Chaucer's *Canterbury Tales* were begun when he was forty-seven and completed when he was sixty-one.
- Verdi wrote his famous and great operas *Otello* at age seventy-four and *Falstaff* at eighty.
- Dr. Lillian Gilbreth was still a paid lecturer at the age of ninety. (I heard her when she was only eighty or so—she was marvelous.)
- And—are you ready?—Titian painted his masterpiece, "The Battle of Lapanto," when he was ninety-eight.

Now what was that nonsense about being too old? Too old for what?

Handicaps

Are you letting your handicaps handicap you?

It is an easy thing to do, isn't it?

I don't and won't minimize your problem for a minute. I do tell you very honestly, however, that I have hired many handicapped persons, but never out of pity.

The ones I hired sold me on their *ability* and mentioned *disability* only as it related to the job.

Honesty also forces me to admit: I turned down many handicapped persons. Why? Usually because I couldn't create a job out of thin air. Sometimes because I concluded the applicant was more handicapped by a poor attitude than by physical disability. Few employers have learned how to turn a poor attitude into a positive one.

What can the handicapped person do to sell himself or herself?

Plenty.

As a start, the handicapped candidate can cite a list of *advantages* to the prospective employer.

Here are some advantages:

- The handicapped person, knowing how difficult it is to find employment in the first place, doesn't move from job to job.
- The handicapped person increases the productivity of others by setting a good example. (I can vouch for this—we once hired a wonderfully talented blind woman for our transcribing division. Her output was tremendous. The added advantage: Others around her increased their output too—by amounts you wouldn't believe.)
- Training is available to the handicapped person by service agencies. This saves the prospective employer many training dollars.

Ask Penetrating Questions:

Your questions should be designed to turn the interviewer's thinking into positive channels with regard to handicapped persons—questions such as:

- How many times have you had to train someone for this position? (The interviewer will conclude that, once trained, *you'll* stay.)
- How often do you go to a worker's place of work only to find the worker off on a break or visiting with someone? (This implies that you wouldn't and couldn't do this.)
- How often have you hired someone who is indifferent to the job?

Where to Go for Help If You're Handicapped:

- to the state employment bureau
- to your board of education for the latest information on training programs
- to your congressman for the latest on special government projects in your area. He or she should know what the Department of Health and Human Services is doing at the moment and is always eager to do something for a voter.

- your church. Usually your minister is truly caring and will go to endless trouble for you. A note of warning: Ministers sometimes are a bit maudlin in your behalf and can put a prospective employer on the spot. This you don't want, for you'll enjoy the job only when you contribute. *And you can contribute.*

Before deciding that your handicap is disabling, remember that James Thurber made drawings he could scarcely see and Beethoven wrote music he couldn't hear.

How to Pass an Employment Test

"Do you mind taking an employment test?"

When you hear that question, rejoice. You are being *actively* considered for a job. Why? Because few employers will suggest a test to a candidate in whom they have little or no interest. Tests consume the administrator's time, and they add to paper costs.

The last time I said as much to a job seeker, the response was a shocked "you've got to be kidding."

Kidding I'm not, but I do understand his reaction. For I hate tests, too. I hate to take them, give them, or score them. I'm not crazy over writing about them either, but this is a must.

Pencils Are Delicious. Think you and I are the only nervous nellies about tests? No, we have company. A lot of it. Ask anyone who has the job of replacing pencils in a testing area. The pencils are not worn. They are chewed.

Tests are still a way of life for the job seeker.

What can you do besides chew your pencil? You can accept the fact that employment tests are still around (although some have been declared discriminatory and abolished). Learning about the kinds of tests you might have to take will make them seem easier. So read on.

Kinds of Employment Tests

General intelligence. The most common tests of general intelligence include:

- **Word comprehension** or **vocabulary tests.** Employers agree that "words are tools of the brain." They are, quite naturally, interested in how you use those tools. So it's not just a matter of knowing a great many words. Your understanding of them is just as important.
- **Reading comprehension** is often part of the general intelligence test. In such a test, you will be asked to read a passage (usually several paragraphs) and then to answer several simple questions that will demonstrate your understanding of what you read.
- **Ability in arithmetic:** Such an ability is necessary in a great many jobs. The British used to refer to an office as a counting house—a rather accurate way of putting it.

  So you see what you do to your chance for employment when you make a sweeping statement against any job involving figures. Alas, almost all jobs do.

  Cheer up. Most arithmetic tests can be handled nicely by a bright eighth grader. Seldom do the questions go beyond fractions, percentages, and decimals. (Bear in mind I'm talking about most tests—not the ones engineers or math majors take.)

  If you apply for a job in a department store, don't be shocked when their test asks, "How many square yards in a nine-by-twelve rug?" Or, "If the tax is 4½ percent, how much will you add to a $20 purchase?" Most manufacturing companies will expect you to know about percentages. So will banks. And almost any employer expects you to be able to add and subtract accurately. So borrow an eighth-grade arithmetic book if you need it.
- **Aptitude tests.** Aptitude tests measure an applicant's capacity for the skills of a specific job or profession.

Aptitude tests can include performance tests such as typing and shorthand. Yes, planning ahead will also help you on these tests.

Let's say you're applying for a job in a real estate office. You can improve your grade considerably if you'll check words that a realtor might include in a shorthand test (i.e., the shorthand symbols for mortgage, lien, or property). If you apply to a bank, think of their terms (actuary, account, interest), and so on, wherever you apply.

- **Personality tests:** These are used to determine whether your personality is suited to a certain type of work. The design of these tests is very ingenious, and there is a great deal of cross-reference. So the word from here is be as honest as you can. Who wants a job for which he or she isn't suited anyway? If there is a way to bone up for these tests, I don't know it.

Spelling. A great many tests of general ability test your skill in spelling. Yes, you can study for these tests in advance. The employment spelling lists are usually *easier* than the ones issued for spelling bees. The same words appear on test after test (accommodate, personnel, embarrassment, and privilege, for example). Suggestion: Get a spelling book at the public library or from a business-school friend or a teacher.

How to Do Well

- Learn about taking tests by looking at tests. The public library has books containing samples.
- Take tests for practice—at your state employment bureau where all kinds of tests are administered (at least at the main branch) for free, and at many schools.

  Take tests anytime a prospective employer offers you the opportunity. No, you don't just waltz in and ask to take their tests. But do accept *every* invitation to take a test. Happy thought: Once in a while, you'll run across a test you have taken elsewhere.

- Learn to read directions: Ask if you have a limited time in which to read directions. If you don't, relax and take all the time you need. If you're told you are not timed, you won't be.

  Get the big picture first. Then reread the directions to be sure you understand. *Ask questions.* Once you start the test, keep moving.
- Tips on true-false tests:
  1. Moderate statements are often true.
  2. Very extreme statements are almost always false.
  3. If the statement is a little bit false, count on the answer being false.
  4. When statements such as "never," "no one," and "always" appear, the statement is probably false.
- Word clues:

  Compare—means you will be talking about *two* things. You will be telling how they are *alike* and how they are *different.*

  Enumerate—list points as though you were counting.

  Describe—tell in words what something is like. Give a word picture.

  Explain—tell what it is, what it does, how it works.

  Discuss—give pros and cons of a question.

  If it is a completion test: that is, if you are to complete a sentence in one word, use only one. Always look at the examples you are shown.

A parting word before you go to take your test: Wear your watch, and take a good pen or two with you, as well as some sharpened pencils. I blush still at the memory of being handed two freshly sharpened pencils when I took my first employment test. I promptly broke the points off *both* of them. What's more, that was *before* I started on the test.

CHAPTER 11

Letters from Readers

How to Answer Interviewers' Questions

Dear Phyllis:
You've had several columns on questions to ask in the interview and about questions to expect. How about a column devoted to answering some of the most commonly asked questions?
I always appreciate your suggestions on how to prepare applicants for the job campaign. Signed: Charles Beaty II

Dear Charles:
We've only space for a few questions. Let's take the most popular ones.

QUESTION: Why did you apply to Widget Manufacturing Company?

POSSIBLE ANSWER: I applied to Widget because I'm impressed with what I've learned about you. For example, the article in the August issue of *Changing Times* strengthened what I've already learned from Darrell Brown in your buying department. (Such a comment can lead to a real discussion of how you can put your skills and training to use at Widget to your *mutual* benefit.)

I remember an applicant who told me, "Well, I looked up, saw your sign, and said to myself, 'Why not?' and came on in." No, I did not hire him nor the one who said, "I got off the bus and there you were."

Another common but poor answer is, "I applied because I need a job." Your need for a job does not guarantee that you're the person to *help* the company concerned. You can shape that into a good answer if you explain that your need for a job will inspire you to competence and hard work.

QUESTION: Have you any experience in this work?

ANSWER: Obviously, the best answer is "yes," followed by a brief explanation of how perfect a fit you are for the job under consideration. The best answers I've received from inexperienced applicants are these:

1. Fortunately, no. So you can be sure I have nothing to unlearn.
2. No, so I take a fresh view of everything. I know I know less than the boss, but I'm trainable.
3. Experience, no. Skills, yes. (His explanation followed.)

QUESTION: What are your strengths?

POSSIBLE ANSWERS: I am motivated; I desire to achieve (supported by evidence). I set targets. I have a goal, an aim; I'm anything but aimless. (Be prepared to tell what your goal is.) Or you might tell about the pride you take in any team or organization with which you're affiliated.

QUESTION: What are your weaknesses?

ANSWER: Proceed with caution here lest you kill the sale. You don't need to search through your history and find some reason for them to reject you.

In this situation you might admit a need for training peculiar to that particular company. You might say, for example, "Although I have a good background in chemical engineering, I would need to learn your processes." An aspiring secretary might say, "Although I've had excellent training, I would need to learn the shorthand symbols for your particular business."

A young man answered me with, "I'm told I work too hard."

Another said, "I'm too hard on myself when I fail to meet a self-imposed deadline." He added wistfully, "I probably need to learn to be as tolerant of myself as I am of others."

QUESTION: What salary do you expect?

ANSWER: There is no one answer to this hot potato. Here are several answers that have worked well. Please don't try to memorize these, but do digest them and improve on them.

1. "While money is important, my future with your company is of greater concern." Then go on with something such as, "You probably have an established salary range for this job. Can you give me some idea of what it is?"

2. "My salary range is $______ to $______." Such a reply gives you a chance to negotiate. If you name an exact figure, you may be high or too low. Worse still, you might be stuck in a lower bracket.
3. "I am competitive with other candidates of similar background."
4. "My salary is negotiable."

It is up to you to learn something about salaries in your area of work (by asking the people who do the work, by asking your librarian for published figures, or by checking with your state employment bureau).

Charles, as you are aware, I don't like all these questions, but they are being asked. Your students are bound to fare well if they practice their answers before they are in the interview situation. Thanks for writing.

Fair—and Unfair—Questions

Dear Phyllis:
I just came from an interview that surprised me. The interviewer asked all kinds of personal questions. I didn't answer all of them, but I probably answered more than I should have. Can you give me any idea of what's considered a fair question and what isn't? Signed: A.E.R.

Dear A.E.R.:
I would have answered all the questions that had to do with my ability and desire to handle the job under discussion. I would have answered *none* that didn't.

Furthermore, I would have reistered my surprise at being asked personal questions. Something such as, "I'm surprised your company would require you to ask that." I'd start by blaming the company rather than the interviewer, that is if I still wanted such a person to hire me. If need be, you can complain to the company president (presidents get their jobs by caring about what goes on). Or, you can write directly to the Civil Rights Commission in your state capital.

Fair questions are questions that are job related and which cannot be used for discriminatory purposes.

Here are some touchy areas that your interviewer should have handled with discretion:

- Age. It is not lawful to require a birth certificate *before* hiring. It is all right to request a work permit (issued by school authorities) for the underage worker. State laws vary. You won't want to lie about your age, because your employer will find out about it after hiring you.
- Address. Specific inquiry into foreign addresses that would indicate national origin are considered unlawful. An employer may ask about your address and length of residence. He may also ask about a previous address in this country.
- Citizenship. Proof of citizenship may be required after hiring.
- Religion. Questions regarding religion or religious holidays are out of line.
- Race or color. Any inquiry that would indicate race or color is unlawful.
- Work schedule. It is all right to ask about your willingness to work a required work schedule. Inquiries about baby-sitting arrangements or about a specific religious holiday are out of line.
- Educational level. A company may legally require specific educational levels only when they are related to job performance.
- Organizations. Questioning applicants about membership in professional groups is permissible as long as inquiries are not phrased in such a way as to elicit information on race, religion, or national origin.

A.E.R., I've touched upon some of the main areas. There are always more guidelines in the making.

Advice for Succeeding in a Sales Job

Dear Phyllis:
Help. I've just taken a sales job—the only job I could get, I might add. I've never thought of myself as a salesman. Do you mind giving me a letter about sales work? It might help others in the same fix. Signed: Hungry Harold.

Dear Harold:
Mind? I'm delighted that you ask.

Harold, you say you have never thought of yourself as a salesman. Please start today.

Now then, about the letter you requested—instead of a conventional letter, how about a letter of the alphabet? Let's use the letter *e*.

I'll hang all my comments on *e*. That way, you'll have an *e*-zier time remembering.

Here are the qualities stressed by sales managers:

- *Enthusiasm* about your product or service should be evident. Some expert sales people use the last letters of enthusiasm, the *i,a,s,m,* to mean I am sold myself.
- *Eagerness* to help customers is necessary. Show them how your product can solve their problems or reduce their costs.
- *Enroll everyone* you know in your campaign.
- *Earliness* is important. Be there ahead of your competitors. Be a self-starter.
- *Examine* the techniques of other salespersons. Examine every ad you see or hear. Are there clues that will help you sell your product?
- *Exude* cleanliness. Your appearance should be exemplary in all ways, including choice of clothing and hair style. Add to this a bright, clean smile.
- *Express* yourself well. Use words that are free of errors in grammar—words that are shiny and fresh.
- *Expose* what you're really like. Let your real self show. When you learn to like yourself enough to be yourself, you'll find that other people like you, too.
- *Extend* yourself. After you've called on your entire list of prospects for the day, call on one more. And remember, it doesn't count as a call if you say to the receptionist, "Here's my card, please ask Ms. Smith to let me know if she has a need for my product."
- *Expect* a certain amount of rejection. When it is planned for, it can be handled more easily.
- *Expect* to succeed.

While we're at it, let me pass along these two sales stories. Both are true.

Henry Ford (I can't remember which Henry) once bought a fabulously large insurance policy. Henry's friend and golf partner (an insurance salesman) read about the purchase with surprise and resentment.

"Henry," he said, "why in the world didn't you tell me you wanted to buy insurance?"

Henry's laconic reply? "You didn't ask."

A salesman called on an unresponsive manufacturer. As the salesman reached the climax of his talk, he began throwing quarters out the window of the manufacturer's office.

"What in the world are you doing?" the manufacturer shouted to the salesman.

"The same thing you are," the salesman responded. "Throwing money out the window."

He made the sale.

Transfer to Another Town?

Dear Mrs. Martin:

Here's one for you. My wife is being transferred out of town. Her job will be over three hundred miles from here so commuting is out. I hate to admit it but her job is better than mine. Now what?

Shall I ask her to refuse the transfer? I hate to give up my present job because it's probably better than a starting one in the new town. To make matters worse, a salary increase goes with her transfer. What do you think? Jake.

Dear Jake:

I think your wife deserves congratulations—from you. She also needs your emotional support.

Suppose you say to yourself, "Okay, the job I have now isn't so special. I might even better myself."

Then, busy yourself with these constructive activities:

- Give your present employer adequate notice. Train a successor. Make notes on how to do your job; also, make notes on how you'd suggest it be done better. Ask your present employer for referrals.
- Ask the placement director of your school or college for referrals. (Never mind that you've been away for a while.

The placement directors know who's recruiting and what jobs are available.)

- Tap the resources of the chamber of commerce in your new town. If the new town is too small to have a chamber, write to the state chamber of commerce.
- Begin your subscription to the town's newspaper. Check their want ads. But don't stop there; also look for articles about local companies on the business pages. That's where you'll find your leads.
- Think about clubs or fraternal organizations to which you belong. Have they members in your new town? How about fellow alumni?
- Check the public library for material about companies or organizations in your new location. Be sure you have searched the periodical review for pertinent information. If you're one of the many who don't know how to do this, ask your librarian for help. While you have her attention, ask her to direct you to the *Editor and Publisher's Market Guide.* This is an annual publication that provides information about transportation, tax structure, banking, names and number of department stores, principal industries, educational systems, and names of newspapers.
- Take advantage of the material in the publication *Urban Family's Budget.* It represents forty metropolitan communities. It is published by:

  U.S. Bureau of Labor Statistics
  200 Constitution Avenue, N.W.
  Washington, D.C. 20210

Jake, if you do all of the above, you won't have time to worry. What's more, you'll have some good job leads.

Fired? Should You Tell the Interviewer?

Dear Mrs. Martin:
I've been fired. Do I have to level with my next employer? How do I handle this in an interview? Signed: Blue Indigo.

Dear Blue Indigo:
Your first three words tell me you are at least facing facts.

Often, people use a lot of high-sounding nonsense to say the same thing.

Yes, do level with your next employer (if you don't, someone else will). But first, level with yourself. If you don't know why you were fired, find out. Say to your former boss, "How can I improve in my next job?" and not "Why did you do this to me?" The first approach may gain an unexpected ally for you.

In the job interview, handle your firing with all the honesty and forthrightness you can muster. Instead of making excuses for yourself, admit your mistakes. Then emphasize what you learned from the experience. Specifically, tell how that knowledge will benefit your next employer.

Your break with your old company may be the best break you ever had. Take some comfort from this: Even some company presidents have experienced being fired, too.

A Parting Word

I'll close this book as I started it by urging you to put your best into the magic formula. Only your best will ensure the best job for you.

On average, the quality of position offered is dramatically higher after your first ten interviews. So, please, don't lose heart—and steam—too soon. The purpose in having you plan for twenty interviews is to increase your opportunity to screen employers. Quite frankly, we've had too much of this one-sided screening. Don't just wait to *be* screened. Screen the employer for a change. You can if you'll remember, the formula is:

1 − 5 + 10 + 15 + 20 = 5 job offers = 1 job, the right job.

Look at page 3 to jog your memory.

Once you get the hang of this job seeking, it can be as much fun as courtship. Well, almost.

Best wishes,
Phyllis Martin

BIBLIOGRAPHY

Career Guidance

Bolles, Richard N., *What Color Is Your Parachute?* Berkeley, California: Ten Speed Press, 1979.

Catalyst, "Résumé Preparation Manual," 1976. Many other publications, too. Available from Catalyst, 14 East 60th Street, New York, New York 10028.

Crystal, John C. and Bolles, Richard N., *Where Do I Go From Here With My Life?* New York: Seabury Press, 1974.

Holland, John L., *Making Vocational Choices: a theory of careers.* Englewood Cliffs, New Jersey: Prentice-Hall, 1973.

Irish, Richard K., *Go Hire Yourself an Employer.* New York: Anchor, 1978.

Jackson, Tom, *Guerrilla Tactics in the Job Market.* New York: Bantam, 1977.

Jackson, Tom, and Mayleas, Davidyne, *The Hidden Job Market: A System to Beat the System.* New York: Quadrangle, 1976.

James, Muriel and Jongeward, Dorothy, *Born to Win.* Reading, Massachusetts: Addison-Wesley Publishing, 1973.

Jameson, Robert J., *Fifty Great Letters Which Won New Jobs.* Verona, New Jersey: Performance Dynamics, 1975, 1976.

Lakein, Alan, *How to Get Control of Your Time and Your Life.* New York: Signet, 1976.

Landers, Ann, *The Ann Landers Encyclopedia, A to Z.* Garden City, New York: Doubleday, 1978. Look under Careers, Work and Vocations; also Adolescence and Work.

Lathrop, Richard, *Who's Hiring Who.* Berkeley, California: Ten Speed Press, 1977.

Lynch, Edith M., *The Executive Suite—Feminine Style.* New York: AMACOM, 1973.

Martin, Phyllis, *Word Watcher's Handbook: A deletionary of the most abused and misused words.* New York: David McKay, 1977.

Medley, H. Anthony, *Sweaty Palms: The Neglected Art of Being Interviewed.* Belmont, California: Lifetime Learning, 1978.

Molloy, John T., *Dress for Success.* New York: P. H. Wyden, 1975. *Woman's Dress for Success Book.* Chicago: Follett, 1977.

Splaver, Sarah, *Nontraditional Careers for Women.* New York: Julian Messner, 1973.

Storey, W.D., "Career Dimensions I—An Exposure to Life Planning and an Approach for Developing a Personal Framework for Career Planning." Croton-on-Hudson, New York: General Electric Company, 1976.

Writer's Digest, *Internships 1981.* Cincinnati, Ohio.

Overseas Employment

Directory of American Firms Operating in Foreign Countries. World Trade Academy Press, Inc., 50 East 42nd Street, New York, New York 10017.

Directory of Overseas Summer Jobs. Writer's Digest Books, 9933 Alliance Road, Cincinnati, Ohio 45242.

Foreign Service List, U.S. Government Printing Office, Superintendent of Documents, Washington, D.C. 20402.

Summer Jobs in Britain. Writer's Digest Books, 9933 Alliance Road, Cincinnati, Ohio 45242.

Summer Employment

Summer Employment Directory of the United States, Writer's Digest Books, 9933 Alliance Road, Cincinnati, Ohio 45242. (See above for summer jobs overseas.)

From the Reference Room of the Public Library

Dictionary of Occupational Titles. Ask to see the latest edition. For sale by the Superintendent of Documents, U.S. Government Printing Office, Washington, D.C. 20402.

Encyclopedia of Careers and Vocational Guidance, Volume II: *Planning Your Career,* Volume II: *Careers and Occupations.* For sale by the Superintendent of Documents, U.S. Government Printing Office, Washington, D.C. 20402.

Guide for Occupational Exploration. For sale by the Superintendent of Documents, U.S. Government Printing Office, Washington, D.C. 20402.

Guide to American Directories. Published by B. Klein, Coral Springs, Florida; Bernard Klein, editor. Information on over six thousand directories covering more than three hundred subjects.

Occupational Outlook Handbook. Ask to see the latest edition. For sale by the Superintendent of Documents, U.S. Government Printing Office, Washington, D.C. 20402.

Standard & Poor's Register of Corporations, Directories and Executives. Published by Standard & Poor's, 25 Broadway, New York, NY 10004.

Standard Rate & Data. Published by Rate & Data Service Inc., Skokie, Ill. Has names and addresses of trade publications in thousands of fields, listed by topic. You might also find a copy in an ad agency.

Thomas' Register of American Manufacturers. Thomas Publishing Company, 1 Penn Plaza, New York, NY 10001. Information about manufacturers and their products.

Unions

Directory of National Unions and Employee Associations. This lists unions and gives the names of officers. For sale by the Superintendent of Documents, U.S. Government Printing Office, Washington, D.C. 20402.

Special Groups

Equipment Manufacturers

A number of companies that manufacture or deal in appliances that require skilled maintenance will help you to secure a position if you know how to use those appliances. This is particularly true of dealers in typewriters, word processors, and other office appliances or equipment. Many large cities have sales offices for typewriters and other office equipment.

Mentally Handicapped

Guide to Job Placement of Mentally Retarded Workers (pamphlet), 1975.
How to Get a Job (pamphlet), 1975.
Jobs and Mentally Retarded People, 1974.
Preparing for Work, 1975.
For any of the above four publications, write to President's

Committee on Employment of the Handicapped, Room 600, Vanguard Building, 1111 20th Street NW, Washington, D.C. 20036.

For Information on Occupations in Demand

"Occupations in Demand." Lists the number of job openings for over one hundred occupations and the cities or localities in which they are available. Revised monthly. Free. Ask for item no. 535H, Consumer Information Center, Pueblo, Colorado 81009. Please note *free* on envelope.

Older Workers

"Educational Opportunities for Older Persons," 1978. Resources for loans, scholarships, and grants for adult education. Free. Ask for item no. 532H, Consumer Information Center, Pueblo, Colorado 81009. Please note *free* on envelope.

"Services for Older Workers," 1977, and "Memo to Mature Jobseekers," 1977 (both are Program Fact Sheets). Both are available from the Office of Information, Inquiries Section, Room 10225, Employment and Training Administration, U.S. Department of Labor, 601 D Street NW, Washington, D.C. 20213.

Physically Handicapped

Careers for the Homebound.

People at Work: 50 Profiles of Men and Women with MS, 1975.

For either of the above two publications, write to President's Committee on Employment of the Handicapped, Room 600, Vanguard Building, 1111 20th Street NW, Washington, D.C. 20036.

Senior Services

Many communities provide services for older job seekers. This is often referred to as a senior job registry. In some areas, those over fifty-five years of age are served, while in other areas service is limited to those over sixty years of age. Your mayor or other elected official can tell you about what exists in your community.

Veterans

Out of the Service and Looking for a Job? Here's Help!, 1976.

Veterans for Hire: Good Business, 1976.

For either of the above two publications, write to Office of Information, Inquiries Section, Room 10225, Employment and Training Administration, U.S. Department of Labor, 601 D Street NW, Washington, D.C. 20213.

Youth

"Employment and Training for Youth" (Program Fact Sheet), February 1977, Office of Information, Inquiries Section, Room 10225, Employment and Training Administration, U.S. Department of Labor, 601 D Street NW, Washington, D.C. 20213.

"Student Guide—Six Federal Financial Aid Programs," 1979. Describes six grant and loan programs for college, vocational, and technical school students. Free. Ask for item no. 537H, Consumer Information Center, Pueblo, Colorado 81009. Please note *free* on envelope.

State-by-State Information

A number of states publish brochures on writing résumés, finding job openings, preparing for interviews, and other aspects of the job search.

In addition, there are state directories that list major industries within their state.

I have compiled these listings under state headings. In each instance, the number 1. refers to the agency furnishing brochures and other material. Number 2. refers to the directory that lists the companies within the state.

You will also want to tap the resources of the chamber of commerce in your state for any needed assistance. Just address the chamber in care of your capital city. You will, of course, check the chamber in your town if one is located there.

Alabama

1. Public Information Officer
   Department of Industrial Relations
   Industrial Relations Building
   649 Monroe Street
   Montgomery, Alabama 36130
2. Industrial Alabama
   Alabama Chamber of Commerce
   P.O. Box 76
   Montgomery, Alabama 36101

Alaska

1. Information Officer
   Employment Security Division
   Department of Labor
   P.O. Box 3-7000
   Juneau, Alaska 99811
2. The Alaska Directory
   A Division of Petroleum Information Corporation
   409 West Northern Lights Boulevard
   Anchorage, Alaska 99503

Arizona

1. Chief of Information and Education
   Arizona State Employment Security Commission
   P.O. Box 6123
   Phoenix, Arizona 85005
2. Arizona Directory of Manufacturers
   Arizona Department of Economic Security
   Unemployment Compensation Division
   P.O. Box 6123
   Phoenix, Arizona 85005

Arkansas

1. Public Information Officer
   Employment Security Division
   P.O. Box 2981

Little Rock, Arkansas 72203
2. Directory of Arkansas Industries
Arkansas Industrial Development Foundation
P.O. Box 1784
Little Rock, Arkansas 72203

California

1. Public Information Section
Employment Development Department
800 Capitol Mall
Sacramento, California 95814
2. California Employment Directory
California Employment Directory, Inc.
580 Market Street
San Francisco, California 94104

California Manufacturers Register
Times-Mirror Press
1115 South Boyle
Los Angeles, California 90023

Colorado

1. Public Information Officer
Division of Employment
Department of Labor and Employment
251 East 12th Avenue
Denver, Colorado 80203
2. Directory of Colorado Manufacturers
Business Research Division
Graduate School of Business Administration
University of Colorado
Boulder, Colorado 80302

Connecticut

1. Public Information Supervisor
Connecticut Employment Security Division
200 Folly Brook Boulevard
Wethersfield, Connecticut 06109
2. Connecticut Manufacturing Directory

Connecticut Labor Department
200 Folly Brook Boulevard
Wethersfield, Connecticut 06109

Delaware

1. Secretary, Department of Labor
   801 West 14th Street
   Wilmington, Delaware 19899
2. Directory of Commerce and Industry
   State of Delaware
   Delaware State Chamber of Commerce
   1102 West Street
   Wilmington, Delaware 19801

District of Columbia

1. Chief, Community Relations and Information Office
   D.C. Department of Manpower, Room 601
   500 C Street NW
   Washington, D.C. 20212
2. Washington, D.C., Manufacturers Directory
   Economic Development Committee
   Washington Board of Trade
   1129 20th Street NW
   Washington, D.C. 20036

Florida

1. Information Director
   Florida Department of Commerce
   Collins Building
   Tallahassee, Florida 32304
2. Directory of Florida Industries
   Florida State Chamber of Commerce
   P.O. Box 8046
   Jacksonville, Florida 32211

Georgia

1. Chief of Public Relations and Information
   Georgia Department of Labor
   254 Washington Street SW
   Atlanta, Georgia 30334

2. Georgia Manufacturing Directory
   Georgia Department of Community Development
   P.O. Box 38097
   100 State Capitol
   Atlanta, Georgia 30334

Hawaii

1. Information Specialist
   Department of Labor and Industrial Relations
   825 Mililani Street
   Honolulu, Hawaii 96813
2. Directory of Manufacturers
   State of Hawaii
   Chamber of Commerce of Hawaii
   Dillingham Building
   Honolulu, Hawaii 96813

Idaho

1. Public Information Coordinator
   Department of Employment
   P.O. Box 35
   Boise, Idaho 83707
2. Directory of Idaho Manufacturers
   Idaho Department of Commerce and Development
   State Capitol Building
   Boise, Idaho 83720

Illinois

1. Director, Communications and Public Information
   Illinois Department of Labor
   State Office Building, Room 705
   Springfield, Illinois 62706
2. Illinois Manufacturers Directory
   Manufacturers News Incorporated
   3 East Huron Street
   Chicago, Illinois 60611

Indiana

1. Director of Information and Education
   Employment Security Division

10 North Senate Avenue
Indianapolis, Indiana 46204

2. Indiana Industrial Directory
Indiana State Chamber of Commerce
Board of Trade Building
Indianapolis, Indiana 46204

Iowa

1. Chief of Information Services
Employment Security Commission
1000 East Grand Avenue
Des Moines, Iowa 50319
2. Iowa Manufacturers
Iowa Development Commission
250 Jewett Building
Des Moines, Iowa 50309

Kansas

1. Public Relations Director
Department of Human Resources
401 Topeka Avenue
Topeka, Kansas 66603
2. Kansas Manufacturers
Kansas Department of Economic Development
State Office Building
Topeka, Kansas 66612

Kentucky

1. Supervisor, Public Information
Department of Human Resources
592 East Main Street
Frankfort, Kentucky 40601
2. Kentucky Directory of Manufacturers
Kentucky Department of Commerce
Division of Research and Planning
Frankfort, Kentucky 40601

Louisiana

1. Public Relations Director
Department of Employment Security

P.O. Box 44094
Baton Rouge, Louisiana 70804

2. Louisiana Directory of Manufacturers
TJM Corporation
P.O. Box 66517
Baton Rouge, Louisiana 70806

Maine

1. Chairman, Employment Security Commission
20 Union Street
Augusta, Maine 04330
2. Buyer's Directory of Maine Industries
Department of Commerce
State Office Building
Augusta, Maine 04330

Maryland

1. Director of Public Relations
Department of Employment and Social Services
1100 North Eutaw Street, Room 601
Baltimore, Maryland 21201
2. Directory of Maryland Manufacturers
Maryland Department of Economic Development
Research Division
2525 Riva Road
Annapolis, Maryland 21401

Massachusetts

1. Supervisor of Information
Division of Employment Security
Hurley Building, Government Center
Boston, Massachusetts 02114
2. Industrial Directory of Massachusetts
Massachusetts Department of Commerce
Public Documents Division
100 Cambridge Street
Boston, Massachusetts 02202

Michigan

1. Director, Information Services Division
   Employment Security Commission
   Department of Labor Building
   7310 Woodward Avenue
   Detroit, Michigan 48202
2. Directory of Michigan Manufacturers
   Harris Publishing Company
   2057-2 Aurora Road
   Twinsburg, Ohio 44087

Minnesota

1. Director of Public Information
   Department of Employment Services
   390 North Robert Street
   St. Paul, Minnesota 55101
2. Directory of Minnesota Manufacturers
   Minnesota Documents Section
   Centennial Building, Room 140
   St. Paul, Minnesota 55101

Mississippi

1. Public Relations Representative
   Employment Security Commission
   P.O. Box 1699
   Jackson, Mississippi 39205
2. Mississippi Manufacturers Directory
   Mississippi Research and Development Center
   P.O. Box 2470
   Jackson, Mississippi 39205

Missouri

1. Information Supervisor
   Division of Employment Security
   Department of Labor and Industrial Relations
   P.O. Box 59
   Jefferson City, Missouri 65101

2. Missouri Directory of Manufacturers
   Division of Commerce and Industrial Development
   Jefferson Building
   Jefferson City, Missouri 65101

Montana

1. Information Officer
   Employment Security Division
   P.O. Box 1728
   Helena, Montana 59601
2. Montana Directory of Manufacturers
   State Division of Planning and Economic Development
   Capital Station
   Helena, Montana 59601

Nebraska

1. Information Officer
   Division of Employment, Department of Labor
   P.O. Box 94600
   State House Station
   Lincoln, Nebraska 68509
2. Directory of Nebraska Manufacturers
   Department of Economic Development
   State Capitol
   Lincoln, Nebraska 68509

Nevada

1. Public Information Officer
   Employment Security Department
   500 East Third Street
   Carson City, Nevada 89701
2. Nevada Industrial Directory
   Nevada Department of Economic Development
   State Office Building
   Carson City, Nevada 89701

New Hampshire

1. Commissioner, Department of Employment Security
   32 South Main Street
   Concord, New Hampshire 03301
2. Made in New Hampshire
   New Hampshire Department of Resources & Economic Development
   State House Annex
   Concord, New Hampshire 03301

New Jersey

1. Director of Public Information
   Division of Employment Security
   Department of Labor and Industry
   John Fitch Plaza
   Trenton, New Jersey 08625
2. New Jersey State Industrial Directory
   State Industrial Directory, Inc.
   2 Penn Plaza
   New York, New York 10001

New Mexico

1. Information Officer
   Employment Security Commission
   P.O. Box 1928
   Albuquerque, New Mexico 87103
2. Directory of New Mexico Manufacturing and Mining
   New Mexico Department of Development
   113 Washington Avenue
   Santa Fe, New Mexico 87501

New York

1. Director, Division of Research and Statistics
   Department of Labor
   2 World Trade Center
   New York, New York 10047

2. New York State Industrial Directory
   State Industrial Directory, Inc.
   2 Penn Plaza
   New York, New York 10001

North Carolina

1. Communications and Information Specialist
   Employment Security Commission
   P.O. Box 25903
   Raleigh, North Carolina 27602
2. North Carolina Directory of Manufacturing Firms
   North Carolina Department of Natural & Economic Resources
   P.O. Box 27687
   Raleigh, North Carolina 27611

North Dakota

1. Publication Information Section
   Employment Security Bureau
   1000 E Street
   Bismarck, North Dakota 58501
2. Directory of North Dakota Manufacturers
   North Dakota Industrial Development Commission
   State Capitol
   Bismarck, North Dakota 58501

Ohio

1. Public Information Officer
   Bureau of Employment Services
   145 South Front Street
   Columbus, Ohio 43216
2. Directory of Ohio Manufacturers
   Harris Publishing Company
   33140 Aurora Road
   Cleveland, Ohio 44139

Oklahoma

1. Information Director
   Employment Security Commission
   Will Rogers Memorial Office Building
   Oklahoma City, Oklahoma 73105
2. Oklahoma Manufacturers Directory
   Oklahoma Industrial Development Department
   Will Rogers Building, Room 500
   Oklahoma City, Oklahoma 73105

Oregon

1. Information Officer
   Employment Division
   875 Union Street NE
   Salem, Oregon 97310
2. Directory of Oregon Manufacturers
   State of Oregon, Department of Commerce
   Economic Development Division
   317 SW Alder
   Portland, Oregon 97204

Pennsylvania

1. Director of Public Relations
   Bureau of Employment Security
   Department of Labor and Industry Building
   Seventh and Forster Streets
   Harrisburg, Pennsylvania 17121
2. Pennsylvania Industrial Directory
   State Industrial Directory, Inc.
   2 Penn Plaza
   New York, New York 10001

Rhode Island

1. Information Officer
   Department of Employment Security
   24 Mason Street
   Providence, Rhode Island 02903

2. Rhode Island Commercial Establishments
   Rhode Island Development Council
   Roger Williams Building
   Providence, Rhode Island 02908

South Carolina

1. Public Information Director
   Employment Security Commission
   P.O. Box 995
   Columbia, South Carolina 29202
2. Industrial Directory of South Carolina
   South Carolina State Development Board
   P.O. Box 927
   Columbia, South Carolina 29202

South Dakota

1. Public Information Director
   Department of Labor
   State Office Building No. 2
   Pierre, South Dakota 57501
2. South Dakota Manufacturers Directory
   Department of Economics and Tourism Development
   State Office Building, No. 2
   Pierre, South Dakota 57501

Tennessee

1. Chief of Public Relations
   Department of Employment Security
   519 Cordell Hull Building
   Nashville, Tennessee 37219
2. Directory of Tennessee Industries
   Department of Economic Development
   1216 Andrew Jackson State Office Building
   Nashville, Tennessee 37219

Texas

1. Public Information Officer
   Texas Employment Commission
   TEC Building

15th and Congress Avenue
Austin, Texas 78778

2. Directory of Texas Manufacturers
Bureau of Business Research
University of Texas
Austin, Texas 78712

Utah

1. Public Relations Director
Department of Employment Security
P.O. Box 11249
Salt Lake City, Utah 84111
2. Utah Manufacturers Directory
Utah Committee of Employment Security
174 Social Hall Avenue
Salt Lake City, Utah 84111

Vermont

1. Public Information Officer
Department of Employment Security
P.O. Box 488
Montpelier, Vermont 05602
2. Directory of Vermont Manufacturers
Vermont Development Commission
State Office Building
Montpelier, Vermont 05602

Virginia

1. Director, Information Services
Virginia Employment Commission
P.O. Box 1358
Richmond, Virginia 23211
2. Industrial Directory of Virginia
Virginia State Chamber of Commerce
611 East Franklin Street
Richmond, Virginia 23219

Washington

1. Information Officer
   Employment Security Department
   P.O. Box 367
   Olympia, Washington 98504
2. Washington Manufacturers Directory
   Washington State Department of Commerce
   General Administration Building
   Olympia, Washington 98504

West Virginia

1. Information Representative
   Department of Employment Security
   4407 McCorkle Avenue S.E.
   Charleston, West Virginia 25305
2. West Virginia Manufacturers Directory
   West Virginia Department of Commerce
   522 Ninth Street
   Huntington, West Virginia 25716

Wisconsin

1. Director of Information
   Department of Industry, Labor, and Human Relations
   P.O. Box 2209
   Madison, Wisconsin 53701
2. Directory of Wisconsin Manufacturers
   Wisconsin Manufacturers Association
   324 East Wisconsin Avenue
   Milwaukee, Wisconsin 53202

Wyoming

1. Information Officer
   Employment Security Commission
   P.O. Box 2760
   Casper, Wyoming 82601
2. Wyoming Directory of Manufacturing and Mining
   Wyoming Department of Economic Planning and
   Development

Barrett Building
Cheyenne, Wyoming 82002

Puerto Rico

1. Information Officer
   Bureau of Employment Security
   414 Barbosa Avenue
   Hato Rey, Puerto Rico 00917
2. Puerto Rico Official Industrial Directory
   Witcom Group Incorporated
   210 Ponce de Leon
   San Juan, Puerto Rico 00901

Reader Notes

For information about television tapes of the eight-part series "Job Seeking—The Shiny Side" featuring Phyllis Martin write: Great Plains Instructional Television Library, Box 80669, Lincoln, Nebraska 68501 or telephone: (402) 472-2007.

If you have job tips you are willing to share, please send them along to me in care of St. Martin's Press, Inc., 175 Fifth Avenue, New York, N.Y. 10010.

....

Mrs. Martin,
Here is a tip that has proved helpful.

____

____

____

Signed: (if you wish) ______________________
Student __________ Education ______________
Age: under 21 ______________ over 21 _________
Occupation ______________ Sex _______________

....

Index